M. NourbeSe Philip

———

Gail Scott

———

Kate Eichhorn

© 2009 by M. NourbeSe Philip, Gail Scott and Kate Eichhorn

All rights reserved. Limited edition. Printed in the USA.

ISBN: 978-0-9764857-8-0

Interior, cover design, & typesetting by HR Hegnauer
Pressed belladonna flower originally found on a Vashon Island beach in Washington State.

  Belladonna* is supported with funds granted by the New York State Council on the Arts and by donations. This book was made possible by FACE OUT, a grant program organized by the Council for Literary Magazines & Presses with the support of The Jerome Foundation and The New York Community Trust. The mission of FACE OUT is to maximize the visibility of emerging writers.

Distributed to the trade by
Small Press Distribution
1341 Seventh Street
Berkeley, CA 94710
www.SPDBooks.org

Also directly available through
Belladonna Books
925 Bergen Street, Suite 405
Brooklyn, NY 11238
orders@belladonnaseries.org

This year marks the tenth anniversary of the Belladonna* mission to: promote the work of women writers who are adventurous, experimental, politically involved, multi-form, multicultural, multi-gendered, impossible to define, delicious to talk about, unpredictable and dangerous with language. Belladonna* has by now featured over 150 writers of wildly diverse age and origin, writers who work in conversation and collaboration within and between multiple forms, languages, critical fields. As performance and as printed text the work collects, gathers over time and space, and forms a conversation about the feminist avant-garde, what it is and how it comes to be. Our anniversary Elders Series is a continuation of this conversation, which highlights the fact of influence and continuity of the ideas, poetics and concerns we circle through.

#6 in the Belladonna Elders Series is Belladonna #123,
published in conjuction with the Belladonna Reading Series at
Dixon Place in New York City, April 14, 2009.

www.BelladonnaSeries.org

M. NourbeSe Philip

———

Gail Scott

———

Kate Eichhorn

BELLADONNA*

2009 · THE ELDERS SERIES · 6

i • PREFACE: THE ELDER FUNCTION

Kate Eichhorn
1 ' *FROM* AUTHOR GESTURE

M. NourbeSe Philip
15 ' INTERVIEW

29 ' *FROM* OROSAN

Gail Scott
53 ' INTERVIEW

65 ' "MACBETH PHYLETIC" *FROM* THE OBITUARY

PREFACE: THE ELDER FUNCTION

The Belladonna Elders Series has proven far more controversial than anticipated. Some critics have charged that the term "elder" is inherently ageist. Others have suggested that the structure of the series reifies problematic notions of artistic lineage. A few detractors have even implied that the Elders Series is symptomatic of a generation of writers unable to invent anew, choosing instead to linger indefinitely as a parasitic presence on their "host" (an older and apparently more vital generation of writers). These objections have arrived from critics speaking across generations and genders. But as Belladonna* curators Rachel Levitsky and Erica Kaufman have repeatedly explained, running counter to prevailing definitions in our culture, the term "elder" is neither synonymous with "old" nor does it signify a stable identitary position.

I came to appreciate the complexity of the elder function during one of my first interviews with a writer in the early 1990s. Maria Campbell, a Métis writer and storyteller, had been invited to speak at a Native elders conference hosted by my university. She graciously offered to spare a few minutes of her time but explained that this *was* an elder's conference, so I would have to conduct the interview in the presence of *her* elders, and because they would potentially be better positioned to respond, she might not speak at all. In the end, this was not an interview with an author but rather an encounter with a writer/storyteller speaking amongst others. I had arrived well prepared, or so I thought, to navigate the complexities of power and appropriation this encounter was bound to raise. I left perplexed, wondering whether I had carried out an interview at all (I don't recall asking any questions). This, of course, is precisely the kind of productive trouble wrought by elders, and for this reason, adopting the category for an avant-garde reading and book series may be surprising, but it is by no means antithetical to the work of a project such as Belladonna*.

Elder, with its radically different ascendency than author, provides an opportunity to pay tribute without demarcating a specific lineage or definitive arrival. Elder and author are both subject positions linked to one's epistemic status, but the conditions under which they are sanctioned to speak, as well as the extent to which they serve legitimizing functions, differ. Neither are universal nor constant, but unlike the elder, the author is a position that can only be realized through an attachment to a text or body of work. The author functions to legitimize texts, determining where and how they can circulate. By contrast, the elder is determined by one's interlocutors. Elder is a position marked by relationality and contingency, welcomingly open to error and slippage. Attentive to the rhythms and realities of everyday life, the elder functions across many and varied terrains. Although it may connote "old" to some, understood in a broader cultural context, its connotations also point to collaborative approaches to knowledge, the possibility of narrative(s) circulating without a single author or origin, and understandings of subjectivity that are not inherently bound up in the individual—in many respects, a set of epistemological and narrative practices far more compatible with avant-garde writing than often appreciated. Significantly, the "elders" featured in this volume, M. NourbeSe Philip and Gail Scott, not only speak to such convergences in the interviews that follow but also exploit them in their contributions to this volume.

Reflecting on the experimental writing community's response to her investigations of imperialism and colonialism through linguistic innovation,

Philip observes, "the Caribbean had postmodernism before the so-called postmodern... in terms of things like bricolage and different discourses... [The writing] comes out of the Caribbean where you have all those interruptions historically. Massive interruptions." Writing from a different geography, but one also profoundly shaped by histories of colonization, Scott's writing reflects a preoccupation with cusps and peculiar fusions. Her new novel, *The Obituary*, investigates the necessity and impossibility of dwelling in such sites. Varied and repeated rituals of contact reverberate at the level of the sentence as French expressions seep into English and English dialogue is delivered carrying traces of an Algonquin language. There are many layers and forms of contamination here; Scott has no investment in purities of grammar or genre.

To be clear, neither Philip nor Scott are exclusively interested in recovering histories that have been placed under erasure or crafting narratives that seek to reify fixed identitary positions. Rather, both writers recognize that colonization naturally gives rise to all sorts of fractured subjects, hybrid forms and polyvalent linguistic registers. By coincidence, their contributions to this volume even share some notable similarities. In their new novels, both writers appropriate popular cinematic and literary genres (Philip adopts the mystery novel and Scott uses film noir as a template). These popular genres are brought into contact with linguistic practices and forms filtered through oral traditions and with discourses pilfered from the ubiquitous canon (Philip's novel is framed by an epigraph from *The Tempest*; the section of Scott's novel included in this volume recasts lines from *Macbeth*). In the way that contact zones often foster narratives marked of interruption, collision and perverse confluences, these texts raise essential considerations about the overlaps between avant-garde writing and some of the other places where fragmentation, parataxis and disjunction are commonplace, and linear narrative and singularity of voice are difficult, if not impossible, to sustain. Perhaps, these surprising parallels reflect the fact that both Philip and Scott write from places where it is more difficult than it is *here* to ignore the prevalence of such overlaps, reminding us that the centre of Empire has never offered the most critical vantage point. I welcome them to the Elders Series as fellow travellers, and as writers whose work has consistently demonstrated to me the immense possibilities pried open when familiar forms and rehearsed paths through the sentence are ruptured.

The nomenclatural debate over the Elders Series may be partially related to a prevailing cultural myopia in experimental writing communities. It may also reflect a reluctance to recognize the achievements of avant-garde women writers who often continue to write despite their writing having little currency in the mainstream publishing world—the apparatus through which authors are produced and sustained. Extending and responding to Michel Foucault's theorizing on the author function, Giorgio Agamben observes that "If we call 'gesture' what remains unexpressed in each expressive act, we can say that… the author is present in the text only as a gesture" (66), but this "illegible gesture" *is* what makes reading possible (70). Whereas reading is a possibility opened up by an "illegible gesture," writing, Agamben suggests, is an "apparatus," and so too is the entire "history of human beings […] nothing other than the hand-to-hand confrontation with the apparatuses they have produced—above all with language" (72). My own contribution to this volume traces these illegible gestures within a distinctly tenuous apparatus—a community of innovative women writers (not unlike the one in which Belladonna* persists). Naturally, my gestures resist representation, and my community lacks any of the geographic or historical specificity that would make this a proper account. My gestures are knowable only through a series of fleeting choreographed encounters. In this scenario, the "elder" functions as stealth vehicle—author and writer, body and imaginary, site where possibilities are both nurtured and subject to interrogation, reminding us that illegibility saturates history and language.

—Kate Eichhorn
March 2009, New York City

Works Cited

Agamben, Giorgio. "The Author as Gesture." *Profanations*. New York: Zone Books, 2007.

Foucault, Michel. "What is an Author?" *Language, Counter-Memory, Practice*. Ithaca: Cornell University Press, 1977.

from AUTHOR GESTURE

Kate Eichhorn

[Horizontal and bruised, but capable of understanding the course of this encounter, sore and traumatized, these ~~private~~ public secrets, I-thoughts corrupting the writing can say she was a name, large enough to be everything, but it's important that nobody knows the author, one of her main functions was being a receptacle, a confidante, action to elevate what contemporariness is, a paradigm not a writer, the fait accompli of this, a ventriloquist, cruelly honest, loving, just being, I suppose, and remembering everything, how we defined, what we did to make ourselves, what we did to be read, always conscious, just sitting and staring, an act of self-creation, part of the process, giving talks on appearances, who was lean, tense, good-looking, useless, unpleasant, the pitch and nervous speed of a given voice or perambulation, the inertia of emotions—she's an infinite line, capable, large enough to be subdivided and still large enough to write, love through waves of shame, hurt, a great release—she was that illusion, a vehicle for my generation, someone I assume might have liked me, incorporated me, a possibility]

How the easily pierced so adeptly reject piercing. Spent her twenties tracking a nipple ring's migration out of the body as if a subcutaneous surface already knows metal doesn't become a drooping torso. Grappling with subjectivities unwilling to fuse the artifice of a woman became a repeated scene splintering until a hard fall for an author function on the cusp of osteoporosis. Felt lack generating desire this libidinal absence was pursued for forthright commentaries on ~~fucking~~ syntax. She was no pervert. This too would be easily dismissed. Time taming the libidinal into a flaccid desire to be simply received. At first how absurd this attraction. The increasing complexity of skin over time. Not an inch without the insistence of accrued cells. How the many stages of calcification restructure the most fluid encounters. Pathological forms threatening to turn entire vascular trees to stone incited fantasies about the pleasure of limits imposed by the lost agility of legs and backs. Natural strictures alleviating expense of garish restraints. Damaged drywall. No pattern could explain this preoccupation with that name appearing on dozen or so bleached spines including one influential genre-defying collection. Another permanently defaced by enthusiastic scrawl exhibiting only rudimentary appreciation for author function's procedures. One reissued across border with hideous tangerine cover. Regrettable author photo. Short hair too long. And with that designation. Classification. That object of study. Pure and simple reconstruction. Afterthought of text. With that possibility. Range of egos. Fictions. Voice animating grids inhabited by figures content to remain plotless. Contemplative. With that mother of all flânerie. Opulent. Witty. Snide figure featured in acclaimed essays on authors series. Voice in freewheeling interview alluding to influence of past lovers on own writing. Shared reading of *The Post Card* in transit with *x*. Unpublished collaboration with *y*. *Zed*'s (or *zee*'s?) syntactical legacy signified by a stretch of uncharacteristically long lines. Always with that risk of desire in philosophical spews. Signature fragmentation. Commingling of obscenity and poetics. Fading signature obtained by a woman when author function approximate age of her now. Prefaced by once cryptic now banal *l'inscription élude l'absence*. At first falling for these dozen or so personae flaunted over decades of publics. In scathing response to review dismissing sixth novel as monotonous. In regrettable self-confessional prose. In fabulous author photo. Leibovitz framing Sontag-like pose. Hands over head. One hand clutching wrist as if taking pulse better to confirm presence than photograph. Half face seized by flash. Guilty. In documentary shot over brunch. Leaning intently into frame declaring narrative rupture in early '80s. Erudite. Not realizing dusting crumbs off blouse. In silhouette at book launch. With translator smoking after taboo. With famous French theorist. Rare expression of disease. In regrettable snapshot looking bloated. Ungenerous institutional lighting. Scarfing back hideously sculpted canapé at university function. Ravenous. With a woman at reading. Right hand on left shoulder. Head tilting down. Caught with bag (or purse?) only thing separating author function's hip from a woman's waist. It could have been any intersection—

> deceptive veins of black ice cross many cities this time of year. The woman is startled by the quickness of her reflexes. The writer by landing. Not the foreignness of new limbs. No regrettable clash of contours. No one insisting on the curvature of their last lover's hip bone

Devastated the woman who had long sought to walk with this exemplary body. Co-opting her stride. Shadowing the certainty—

> because some things aren't structured by eras. There are limits to the historically contingent. Contact so variable

Skirting verdicts they staged their encounters in a rotation of cities. Honoured time restrictions. One day for domestic. Imposed a three day maximum on foreign locales. Emails exchanged under pseudonymous handles stripped down to nouns. Migrated to host languages. Agreed to never finish each other's sentences. Vigilantly policed references to past lovers. Placed moratoriums on souvenirs. Affected items of clothing. Nothing to discredit the present. Nothing lent or traded. Remained selfishly possessive of moments. The claustrophobic anticipation of a darkened cab. Scenes of entry. Two small rooms more intimate than one large. Chose to exploit reservations transforming the impact of adjacent—

> interruption. A repository gratefully relinquishing the unrealized.
> Room for inevitability

Learning more than expected from the writer's inventiveness temporarily severed sex from politics. *Don't!* An illocution not narrative prompt. Unfeministly agreed to repress traumas. Histories. What they had rarely achieved fucking thrived by constraint. After years of seriality discovered a range of new openings. Gathering strands of hair away from damp forehead at 3:00 a.m. Naked and inflamed awaiting application of prescription cream (no point placing strictures on bodies so openly prone to rupture). Fiercely protective of each other's dignity tapped into a capacity for nurture previously unknown. The woman wiped up. Awakening as usual against a cascading sheet of arm. No explanation for the sequence of turns habitually leading back to this precise location. In turn the writer learned to reserve judgment. Withholding a litany of objections centred on grammar. Substitution of ums with likes. Also unforgivable historical inaccuracies. And the woman patiently refrained from silencing the writer's incessant mumbling. Ongoing dialogue with self perfected over decade of solo habitation. The writer refrained from commenting on the woman's cavalier attitude toward capitalization. Deplorable pronunciation. Awkward import of theory into vernacular. The woman learned to ignore growing frequency of pee breaks. Need to think about pee charting routes through Madrid and Rome. Circumnavigation of museums and monuments imposed by inexhaustible streams of urine. The writer refrained from imposing rules on the woman's incessant message checking. Use of cellphone as computer. Pecking vowellessness in airport lounges and hotel lobbies. The agonizing withdrawal. These scheduled intervals too precious for tedious rounds of objection kept their most unlikely affair intact well beyond the one year and seven months they had previously known—

> intimate gestures recast a half-dozen senses. Vibrations through an organ. Light filtering muscle. Shifting modalities

At first perplexed by such forwardness touching so everything merged preempted by living. Desiring the impossible ground across this channel there were some things they would never share. Nostalgia for the same set of objects. Bodies. Eras. They would achieve a sense of sadness. Inauthentic lives lived for the possibility of narrative. Imagined returns. Another version. Recycled mattress. The woman was not the sole object of the writer's gestures. The writer an aperture leading as if desire and mourning are never inseparable. Felt this a devastating blow. Watched a documentary on the perils of years navigating sadness. Many reruns. Preferring pedestrian performance to the entrapment of film played voyeur from hotel windows framing a nexus of marks. Lifetime of external images. Figure constituted by a cycle of sleep and waking treated as a raw surface. Spoken wear and tear attesting to a face. Man shuffling between a slit of green drapery body telling something about augmented survival. Socks and underwear in the kitchen a cardboard cutout hunched over refrigerator contemplative horizontal iridescent empty. The woman placed dibs on a poet. The writer on dementia. Shared a cigarette through a crack in the window spilling ashes onto pigeon droppings. White on white an idol trapped in a monitor surveying carnage. Contemplating a shadow appendage joystick infinite accumulation of experience. Interval. A man washing his face ordered Thai. Agreed it tasted better with chopsticks although inauthentic. Nearly missed an exhibitionist eating something from a bowl half hard speculated on disintegration of private life. Channel surfing irreversible time of articulation individual as portrait possession—

abstract totality typifying the medium, light splices the boulevard on angle distinctive to this time of year. Motorcycle through their line of vision. The writer places her hand on the woman's shoulder. Hand slipping down her arm not a public act of affection this motor drilling. She thinks it's the motorcycle or a scooter burrowing through her skull. Another distinctive angle slices her retina. *n*—the woman calls a name. Entirely unfamiliar. Misinterpellation pushes her away. The woman is hurt. The writer oblivious. Not a resistance to nurture. Remembering her daughter's second birthday, a thunderstorm, the prevalence of polyester, charcoal. Everyone is hairier there but the woman is not in this scene. Horizontal, there's something about the appearance of the sidewalk that magnifies its textures. Ability to hold shadows better than other surfaces. Unappreciated complexity of an aggregate and she loses her for good. Altogether too recent a woman is kneeling on the sidewalk altogether too incidental. Not worrying about impending explanations. From now on a woman will be mistaken for other lovers. Take this as a compliment (most of the time). Waiting for them to arrive a woman is just visiting. Now it's sunny again and her daughter doesn't appreciate the effort. There's a man speaking German. Too young to know her mother hates parties. They're on the bike path and must move. She wonders why she invited a half-dozen two year olds and bought hats. Misinterpellation says something in English with a trailing suffix. She always carries a Band-Aid in her purse on this shoulder that has slipped into the aggregate holding up her body. A woman drags her off the bike path repeating a single short consonant. Author function's daughter is too young to know the party is about someone else on the beach. It's not the charcoal she recognizes. The short consonant is beginning to sound familiar but dated. A woman is part of this scene. Altogether too peripheral to be stroking her forehead altogether too tenuously strapped into this bus. *n*-ing her softly in this vessel I will call a friend on the coast and ask for x's number. It will be 5:00 a.m. Three hours later in x's time zone some German will hang off my French. There will be fewer politics than usual conceding to my imperialist tongue as I tell x what happened after the motorcycle avoiding her name forced through a collapsing mouth on the sidewalk. The American nurse with the hair will sit across from me translating questions into the late afternoon. In the morning x will have forgotten most of her family history, because they're no longer talking. Offer to call author function's daughter. Suggest a meeting on a train and stroll along the wall with a group of tourists longing for Cold War binaries to explain everything after the motorcycle. x will prove astonishingly compassionate without compromising her disapproval at this early hour. I will feel x relieved not to be here in the late afternoon with the displaced nurse filling checkboxes in German. A woman is watching her. She is growing accustomed to repeated short consonants. Permits a hand through a matted clump of hair, but has no idea how she knows her husband, who spends too much time in the field with metal scraps and a camera. A woman assures her this isn't cancer.

Disappointed she's wasted decades on paranoia. Appreciates the arms hoisting metal into temporary structures until her daughter falls again on a fragment. Hates her husband. Always carries a Band-Aid in her purse on this shoulder sinking into the bleached fabric. A woman assures her there are many Band-Aids in this building and she doesn't need one, but she knows her daughter's bleeding and her husband's an idiot. She's panicked with a woman's lips on her forehead in this bed frame. Put out by the thought of driving to town for a tetanus shot. Everything feels inappropriate here. x will ask the daughter to call me. It will be awkward despite the train and the wall. Author function will never be spontaneous or have a pension. I will avoid the purse and the Band-Aids. Turning 40 three days after the motorcycle, the daughter will recall herself naked in a red plastic cooler watching her mother smoke a joint in the shade. She asks her daughter about a woman, but it's x again breaking syllables in a completely foreign language. Reminds her of the table discovered on a roadside. She knows this is after the fragments of metal and before a woman, before an oscillating line charting her progress. Breaking syllables in a completely foreign language reminds her of an oscillating line charting her progress. Unheimlichs abounding, author function confronts a litany of familiars. The varnish worn off only half the table prompted six years of speculation on variable wear (their only successful authorial collaboration). x describes the shade and pattern of their ceramics, adjusts the phone, hinge never fixed on cupboard. Recites recipes, omitting titles and instructions: 3 cups dry red wine, 2 cups beef stock, 1/4 cup cognac. Author function wonders if they'll serve pudding. Onions, garlic (cadence more irritating than remembered), thyme. x claims to miss a hip bone. The comfortable distance between their offices. Tells her she can have the lamp back. 1 dried bay leaf. Still preoccupied with peripherals, spices, the texture of luncheon meets and distant cousins, x regrets destroying the photographs and personally inscribed books—

for making me, for being here, for being a mechanism
for everything, for everything else, for telling
honing courage, shamelessly loosening hold on the past
for shared readings, for reading in a compelling way, for coming
to the rescue, for coming of (f) course, for being here
at the advent of 54, socks and oatmeal, taking out the recycling
for patience, virtuosity, imagination, an intensively caring approach
for the limited utility of seriousness, thoughts on enjambment
structure, discernment, for being critical, immeasurably possible
impossible, for being and telling and for being incisively patient, trusty
foe, for the cruelties of true friendship, for pointing this out
for being ~~perfect~~ *perfectly harsh, the provocation of your work*
for the efficacy of remains, for being there
this book owes much to x —

How absurd these enthusiastic spews. Preoccupations hurled on her appearing on a fleeting stretch of inaccessible expressions. Author function surveys a woman. Insistence of short haired woman is the artifice of an acquired taste. Watches her talking. Streams of live performance symptomatic of mourning something real. Gestures overpower her body. No longer deployed or deployable author function relaxes. Prefers this part of the story. Between what is a slit of dialogue, publics in a body threaten egos. Author function wonders how this incited a novel. Prone to anticipation a woman is here as if inseparable from small rooms. More intimate. Author function appreciates her eye for detail. Seams. The most fluid cusp of encounter a woman looks at her. A public act remembering her complexity. A name. Not entirely something about the writer. Author function regrets forgetting formulas but this burrowing heightens her senses. In a park, a container for their very small room, a woman will appear less awkward, less boy. A woman will become the source of the glass-like texture of a ledge intimacy draws out. Implicit minimalist interaction rewrites the story to her—

Gesture 1 Monumentality, archway, wall. Varied acts of selection. Touching: another function. Provocatively, having a crush is all about texture.

Gesture 2 Testament to intimacy and attachment: single photograph of duality. To be useful, surfaces ignore what actually is.

Gesture 3 The incommunicable movement from closeness to a revolution made of gritty intensity. Awareness of scents. Monotonous vibrating note after separation. The writer is mature enough to include these details. She *has* fucked a woman in her park.

Gesture 4 Embodiment (a woman can't spend all her time theorizing another generation's writing).

Gesture 5 Bodies pouring scandal feel too course to be openly affectionate in public. Author function assures her it's dusk. Hiplessness and attitude, she'll be read as a boy. Be the recipient of another glass of wine to keep up with the demands of this exchange

>**Subject: Re: Author Gesture**
>**Date:** Tuesday, April 14, 2009 3:54 PM
>**From:** NL <authorfunction@gmail.com>
>**To:** KE <thewriter@gmail.com>

>**Subject: Re: Author Gesture**

>>I've never resorted to banal inscriptions. why state inscription eludes one's
>>absence when obvious? derivative. Had I signed said book, the inscription would
>>be derivative of myself, not Derrida, and I've never had bad hair, not really, and
>>there's no "regrettable self-confessional prose" in my archive, no crumbs on
>>blouse, no documentary shot over brunch. any public smoking took place before
>>not after taboo, and I've never been a voyeur, ravenous, not visibly. I've never
>>been self-absorbed, paranoid or completely subsumed by a love object. there
>>was one successfully co-authored book with a lover, but I would never let
>>a lover influence my line length, generic conventions, the pace or range of a sentence,
>>and I've never had an affair with a younger woman (not that young!). there was
>>an exhusband -- a playwright, not a sculptor (where did you dig up the sculptor?).
>>no daughter -- a son who'd never be here. You never mentioned the folk singer, the
>>Buddhist or the archivist... thanks (if intentional?). btw, Ive never carried Band-Aids
>>and rarely carried a purse. there have been many bags, briefcases,
>>knapsacks, I'll admit, even a series of appropriated baskets. And what's with the
>>moralizing rant on smoking pot and child rearing? Everyone was less anal back
>>then. I like the part about being an exemplary flaneur but there have been no broken
>>bones, no cascading sheets of arm -- I've always taken care of my triceps. About
>>the book blurb, I'm busy but I'd like to do it, so let me get back to you in a week or so.
>>best, n

>>On 18/05/08 11:17 PM, "K E"<fromthewriter@gmail.com>
>><http://thewriter@gmail.com> wrote:

>>Dear n, I am writing to ask if you would be willing to blurb my book. The timeline

Author function notices the presumptuous placement of a woman's hand on her shoulder at the reading. I feel this intrusive, comforting, subsuming. The affect and complicity. Familiar and refined, a philosopher takes author function's place genderless at the microphone. Lascivious in her frustrating multilingual desire. Acclaimed sexless European lover a pixilated torso dismantling in the front row. During the break a half-dozen others perform on stage. I sit next to a poet with a pungent recitation and big head. Many fit this description. Tonight author function attends her own reading because I'll never pull off hysterical realism, tears or thigh-high boots. Flattened, I remain seated. Later seep out and recall watching a speechless sofa, a wall and series of awkward introductions.

M. NourbeSe Philip

Interview with M. NourbeSe Philip

Toronto, September 2008*

Kate Eichhorn: I've had a recurring conversation with women writers of my generation about the impact of first reading "Discourse on the Logic of Language" in *She Tries Her Tongue*… That a poem could take this form was significant, but more importantly, it demonstrated that sometimes the most politically urgent writing necessitates innovation at the level of language and form. "Discourse on the Logic of Language" couldn't have taken any other form.

M. NourbeSe Philip: Of course not. But one of the things you have to understand, for a poet, most of the payoff comes after you do it, at least for me, the payoff comes in what the work begins to teach you. So let's take "Discourse on the Logic of Language," for instance. I was very aware of how I wanted it set up.

KE: Why?

NP: Because for me when I work in English, I always feel as if I am working in a foreign language.

KE: Even with your mastery?

NP: I never ever take it for granted. The source of the foreignness is the awareness that this is not my tongue. Mind you, I think that all writers and

---

* Excerpt from interview forthcoming in Kate Eichhorn and Heather Milne, eds. *Prismatic Publics: Innovative Canadian Women's Poetry and Poetics*. Toronto: Coach House Books, 2009.

poets have this sense. As you write your poem, you have this idea of perfection, but of course, what I am talking about is slightly different from that. I'm talking about this sense of utter foreignness in what is supposed to be my mother tongue. When I was working on the poem, I remember sitting in this room on St. Clair Avenue in Toronto that I rented from a doctor, my doctor in fact. I had a room at the back of his office, and there were some days when I felt that I could actually taste the foreignness of these words. I can't apply profound theoretical language to it. I can only go to the body and tell you what it felt like. There was this awareness of that and all I could do was weep and weep. Maybe it was some sort of collective memory.

KE: Since you've raised this, I want to ask a question I thought about asking first, but it seemed like a very negative place to begin here—do you love language, or is language just a site of struggle for you?

NP: No! I love it, I love it, I love it! More than that there is an erotic aspect to language for me. As a child, I used to listen to my parents talking about politics on the front porch, while I sat inside doing my homework. There was something very powerful—even erotic for me—hearing the weaving together of my parents' voices—my father's deep and sombre, my mother's higher and more active. I get excited by grammar texts—how weird is that?

KE: So when you think about your work as a poet, are you breaking the language, rupturing the imperialist language, taming the language, redeploying the language?

NP: I'm doing all those things. In fact, when writing the last book of *Zong!*, as I was breaking those words open, I remember feeling, yes, finally, I am fucking with this language in a way I have wanted to do all my life!—my writing life, that is. And an interesting metaphor given what I just said about the erotic. Simultaneous with that, I felt a deep sense of satisfaction—as if I were getting my own back on this language that had fucked us over for so long. That had held us in its grip demanding mastery when we could never be master or mistress even of our own bodies. It was an incredible experience. I finally felt that for the first time I had my own language. True it's fragmented and broken, but it is my own tongue. This totally ruptured, fragmented, dissonant language that is my mother tongue.

KE: But the project of *Zong!* begins a long time ago, before *Zong!* It's all your writing.

NP: I'm thinking of the last poem in my first collection, *Thorns*, and I think the title is "All that Remains of Kush Returns to the Desert." It's a poem addressed to Nyame, a West African deity. The closing lines are something like, "welcome me gently, I carry tiny thorns of Africa within." That whole idea of thorns—the thorniness of it—that language is not something comfortable and comforting, but something that can hurt you, that can maim you. So, that is the closing image in the first book. I think the thorns are still there when I look at *Zong!* I don't even know at this point how to pronounce some parts of the text, particularly in the last section—Ferrum. Do I pronounce each linguistic fragment as a part of the word it has been broken off from or do I allow each fragment its own sound. There is a challenge in getting my mouth and tongue around these pieces. How do I begin to express the brokenness, the fragmentation that is at the heart of this book.

KE: This makes me think about the reading I invited you to do last April. I said, "This time, NourbeSe, don't explain the text, just read." I love your essays, but you are possibly one of the only poets I know of who has consistently chosen to preface or conclude their books with essays. Similarly, you often open or close or interrupt your readings with this other voice. It's always a reading, a lecture and a talk. What was it like to just read and hold back any explanation?

NP: It was exciting. I had never done it quite that way before. Mainly, because I felt that the work was so new to me, it would be new to the audience as well, and I would have to explain it.

KE: I want to talk more about your experience of reading *Zong!* You've already talked about trying to give this text a voice, which is a text you are simply relaying because it's presented as an "as told to" narrative rather than something you authored. But have you also thought more about how you will deal with, and force your listeners to grapple with, its silences?

NP: I did one reading at the Scream Literary Festival in Toronto where I just took two pages and read them quite slowly, honouring the silence, which is really counter intuitive for me, because I am very speedy. It's also counter intuitive in this age, and in certain literary contexts like performance poetry where everything is really, really fast, although that has its validity too. The two pages took about ten minutes to read, but just before the end of that reading, feeling a bit nervous, I sped up. Someone who had been in the audience remarked to me a few days later that it really worked as a slow reading and the audience only seemed to get restless when I sped up. Then, I did another reading in Tobago in July, and this was a totally different context. Tobago is still a very oral society and this was a very small reading—some ten to fifteen people. I think I read two pages again honouring the silences, and once again people were absolutely receptive. Afterwards, one woman said that she felt the silences created images of water washing up on the shore and washing back. Another person said the silences conveyed to him a sense of being under water, drowning. So those two readings really confirmed for me that that is how I should read the text. But I am still working on the pauses and how long those should be.

KE: But that is not how you had imagined reading this text originally. There is an excessiveness about *Zong!* It's a long poetry book, nearly 200 pages, and there are many words on each page. It's also typographically expansive. So to do a twenty-minute reading and only read four pages is a radical act, but it also seems to reiterate that the story can't be told in its entirety and that you aren't going to give it to us.

NP: Exactly, that can't happen with *Zong!* Usually, I get nervous about readings, but since I've understood that that is how I have to read it, it seems fine. It grounds me. Two pages, four pages, is fine. I would like to read the entire text and see how long it takes.

KE: Have you imagined what kind of space this sort of reading could take place in?

NP: I am trying to imagine it. I see it as a space where people could come and go as they please. The reading I did in Tobago was held at a fort in the main town, Scarborough. It's now a historical site and museum and so a destination for visitors. As I was reading on the gallery or porch of this museum, off to my left I could hear the voices of the visitors. It was dark out, but I could make out shapes of people. I thought it fascinating, because I felt that this is how it must have been. On the ship—while people were being thrown overboard, the life of the ship would have gone on. One of the audience members, the same man who told me about the sensation of drowning, mentioned those voices as well and thought that they fit with the reading. Usually, when you are doing a reading and you hear other voices or sounds, it's distracting, and you think that they shouldn't be there. But it felt right somehow—those sounds—and they underscored how other people's lives continued as this horrific act was unfolding. But this is no different from what happens today—just think of how our lives continue as Beirut burns; Iraq disintegrates and we buy lattes; Congo implodes as we speak, and we shop or attend the movies…

KE: It seems that the life of this text has a visual presence that tells one story, but its oral presence tells, and will tell in each context in which you read, a slightly different story as well.

NP: It's interesting, because the two readings I did this summer were to very different audiences. The one here was an audience of poetry aficionados, but the audience in Tobago was not, and yet both responses shared a willingness to listen to the silences and respond to them.

KE: The reading you did at the Scream Literary Festival in Toronto was part of a panel on "appropriation art." But do you even think about a work like *Zong!* as a form of appropriation art or understand the materials you work with as found materials in the same way that some of the other writers on that panel, like Kenny Goldsmith, do?

NP: I'm hesitating… the phrase that comes to mind is "the hard kernels of silence." The legal text of *Zong!* is a hard kernel of silence, because locked in that text is the story of those unnamed Africans who like many, many have been erased from history or memory. For those like myself who try to understand and negotiate the history of colonialism, postcolonialism, neo-colonialism, it is often a zero-sum game. Although it's not a game. It's a process of trying to piece the self back together. So, no, it's not the same process, like taking the *New York Times* and turning an issue into a book. The starting point is different and the stakes are higher. And in trying to negotiate those lacunae, those gaps, you become aware that you can never ever fill them except with the bones. But that panel wasn't a context in which to talk about that.

KE: But that's a problem—the fact that you didn't even feel there was a context in which to talk about those issues. There are poets, of course, who choose a constraint and the book comes out of their chosen constraint or set of constraints, but I have a strong sense that you have never chosen to work with constraints. Would you choose a constraint-based poetic practice if you didn't have to?

NP: In a word, no, but I have always been interested in the idea of limitation and its potential resources. But was that interest a result of my own history? Who knows? What is more interesting to me, however, is an insight about limitations or constraints I gained from the process of writing *Zong!* One of our founding cultural myths in the West is that of freedom—we can do or say anything (within certain constraints, of course); we are free to go out and find our constraints, poach on other cultures and so on. What I began to understand is that even when we think we are freest, if we lift—I want to say that veil of freedom—underneath will be found many unspoken constraints. In my own case, for instance—had I set out to write this work in the way I usually do, I don't think I would have been particularly interested in a white, male European voice. Why? Because the voices of Africans have been so silenced, so erased that it's important to bring those voices forward. But, lo and behold—didn't a white, male voice not surface in the text, unbeknownst to me and without so much as a by your leave. And really it is his trajectory that gives shape such as it is to the book. He comes to realize that he is engaged in a great sin—I use the word advisedly because that is how they thought in those days, and it drives him crazy. Maybe a better way to put it is that he comes to understand that he has moved himself outside of his age where it was acceptable to enslave another human being and transport them thousands of miles—he enters another space/time if you will—we could call it a fugue state—and he realizes that he has to kill himself. That is how he signals both his rejection of his society and his commitment to the Other—those who were being thrown overboard. There is no way I would have been interested in that voice, and although the voice doesn't overwhelm the work, I am very aware of it.

KE: So where did he come from?

NP: He surfaced. He surfaced in the text. What that showed me is that I too have these limitations—these built-in constraints. One of them was that as an African-descended Black woman, I should only be interested in the Black woman's or Black man's story. So how "free" am I really, how lacking in constraint am I, if even with my so-called exercise of choice I am already limiting or constraining myself? What about the constraint—in the form of expectations—that the poetry by African-descended poets should primarily be about certain topics—resistance, revolution; or the belief that we don't as a rule write experimental, avant-garde or innovative poetics? These are all constraints that we either take on or embrace. And could we not argue that the very idea of the freedom to choose a constraint signals the existence of—to use insurance language—pre-existing constraints and serves to mask them by the very idea of freedom to choose the constraint? Further, the apparent absence of constraints in certain groups, which requires one to go out and find one, dovetails nicely with—actually depends on the over abundance of constraints in the lives of others—constraints of gender, class, sexuality and race—constraints which the white, straight male sees himself as outside of. Which is what I think you were getting at with your question. Except that I think the constraint begins a lot earlier than the act of artificially seeking a constraint.

KE: So you couldn't excise his voice even after it came to the surface?

NP: Because it is as much his story as my story. And he represents an idea and a way of being that has to die—drown itself, self-immolate in order for us to reclaim our "is-ness."

KE: I've always read your poetic project as an epistemological project. Who is authorized to know? What can we know? So the fact that this "authorized" knower emerges seems completely appropriate, but so too is the necessity of his death, which in turn authorizes you to tell the story that can't be told.

NP: Of course, it is interesting that he is telling the story through this other figure, Setaey Adamu Boateng, whom I believe is African, and you know in this type of discourse it is usually the white person who tells the story on behalf of the Black person who, for any number of reasons, cannot or isn't allowed to tell the story. In the case of *Zong!*, it is the African woman recounting this story that cannot yet must be told, and within that telling, among the many other stories, is the white man's story.

KE: There is, in the context of innovative poetics, especially in the U.S., a long tradition of poets engaging in a Buddhist practice. So there is a discussion initiated by people like Anne Waldman, and many of the writers who have been associated with the scene at Naropa, about spirituality and innovative poetics, but it seems to be limited to—if I can say it?—mostly white poets who have adopted Buddhism. It seems to me that even if you are not necessarily a religious person, spirituality is also important to your poetic practice. Often when you read, you perform a ritual at the beginning of the reading... are you comfortable talking about this aspect of your writing?

NP: Yes and no, but it is an important question. I think your point is well taken, because even Christianity—the West's own religion—is verboten, isn't it. I think what has to be remembered in terms of this work, *Zong!*, is that spirituality (I hate that word) and religion permeate it. The age, the 18th century, was one in which religion was central to life, hence the mention of sin above. The church, Catholic and Protestant, was deeply involved in the Trade. Indeed, it was a priest, Bartholomew de las Casas, who suggested that in order to stop the destruction of the aboriginal populations of the New World, "negroes" should be imported to do the work in the mines and on the plantations. The rest, as they say, is history. So, religion is both a backdrop to this story. Now, regarding art and spirituality, I think it's important to recall a significant moment in art history—I'm now talking about visual art—when Picasso and other modernists come upon the aesthetics of Africa and Oceania. Hal Foster, the art critic, writes that when the Europeans attempted to engage from these areas, they were unable to deal with the spirituality that was integral to the production of what I'll call cultural artefacts, so they appropriated the form. This was the tradition that saved Western art, infused it with new life, but its spirituality and the chance to reclaim a ritual function for art was explicitly rejected. What, if any, impact did that rejection of spirituality have on Western art? That could be the subject of an entire conversation. But I think one effect is that—and here we come back to constraints again—only certain traditions are allowed in poetry—Taoism (the long shadow of Pound), Buddhism, Zen, but not Christianity and certainly not African spirituality. And, what the hell is that anyway—African spirituality? I say it that way because the average person—African or non-African—doesn't know what it is and many—African peoples included—are afraid of it and see it as part of demon worship. It is interesting that without a church, a written liturgy, a clergy, and in the face of extreme persecution, African belief systems took root in the New World and continue to flourish in places like Cuba, Brazil and Trinidad. Yes, many things happened during the course of writing this work for which I don't have a language to explain. And the modernist, avant-garde, innovative poetics discourse was of no help explaining this either. What I do know, however, is that there was a competing spiritual system, vis-à-vis Christianity I mean, aboard the ship—the ship as I imagined it, that is—and that that system was African. It's interesting that there is this discomfort with spirituality, but there is a sense, and this is somewhat clichéd, in which art has become our new religion—there are no contemporary churches, for instance, that can compete with buildings being presently constructed to house works of art. High priests and disciples—we have them. I could go on, but I think you get my point.

KE: I'm thinking that we could say that there is something aleatory about *Zong!*, since you keep telling these stories about things just happening or appearing that changed or shaped the text, but we might also say, no, that's not it at all. It's not aleatory but rather some other kind of intervention. So my question is how do we think about the difference between a text's aleatory and spiritual elements, or is the aleatory one of those terms we've adopted in the world of avant-garde literature and art to obfuscate what could otherwise be understood as spiritual?

NP: I know that you are not at all meaning this, but I do get a little anxious when the idea of aleatory is linked to work by an African artist. There is a long history of this belief in some natural African or Negro talent that just happens—particularly in the performative arts. Like natural rhythm, it doesn't need training or discipline. For instance, instructions were given—I don't recall all the details—not to direct Robeson in one of the plays he did because you didn't want to affect that instinctive natural Negro talent. Having said that, however, I am aware of trying to hide some of my understanding of the deep spiritual elements of the text, partly because I don't have the language and also because I think that if I talk about it people might misunderstand it or think it is too "new-agey." Of course, I, and we, do ourselves a disservice because poetry's roots are deeply sacred, embedded in ritual, in chants and spells, and all those practices that in another context would be seen as "religious" or "spiritual." This harks back to my earlier comments about visual art. As you well know, I am not Christian, and this is not a brief for bringing the religious into poetry, but merely to look at what constraints we operate under as we write as "free subjects."

KE: Do you feel the need to conceal the spiritual elements of the text across the writing communities you inhabit or just in the context of experimental writing communities?

NP: Definitely in the context of the experimental community—the offshoot of high modernism—but I think it's more widespread than that. Maybe that's something I have to come to terms with. Maybe that is the next step for me? I do want to add, however, that the very idea of concealment is deeply rooted in the historical experiences of enslaved Africans—you may have heard of the idea of hidden in plain view as it applies to the spirituals and quilts produced by African Americans which contained secret messages about fleeing slavery. There was also concealment of spiritual knowledge even from one's own children for fear of betrayal and punishment. And finally the idea of concealment and secrecy is deeply embedded in continental African cultures and practices—the idea that knowledge is only passed on when you are ready for it or only to men or women. It is helpful and productive for me to engage with these ideas around concealment and secrecy rather than seeing my practices of concealment as primarily a negative consequence of working in a commodity-driven art environment bereft of ritual or spirit. It also continues over the idea of the code which I think permeates *Zong!*

KE: Many people have been anticipating *Zong!* since you started to read from it several years ago. But how do you think it will be taken up in experimental writing communities? Or are they even prepared to take up this text?

NP: I think, as you say, it is so excessive on the surface it might prove difficult for people to enter—I hope not. When *She Tries her Tongue...* was published people talked about it as being a postmodernist text, and I didn't have a problem with that, but many of those people didn't understand the Caribbean and the postcolonial aspects of the area and the text. They also didn't understand how the Caribbean was postmodern long before postmodernism. Because in terms of things like bricolage and competing discourses, they were already there, and that is where that text comes from—it comes out of the Caribbean. With *Zong!*

I suspect people will first see its experimental nature and its relationship to the modernist traditions, but in its use of competing motifs and stories, I see links with certain aspects of Yoruba aesthetic practices. I suspect it will take a longer time for readers to see that.

from O<small>RO</small>S<small>AN</small>

M. NourbeSe Philip

PROEM

Waves break as if out of nothing. Against the black sea white lace froths. The urgent rush of water up the beach is balanced by the soughing sound of a less hurried return. The moon, past its fullness by some two or three days, appears from behind a cloud to silhouette two figures on a deserted beach; they stand about fifty feet apart. Slowly, even tentatively, they move toward each other; soon they are running, and where once there were two bodies, four separate limbs, there now exists one unit joined at mouth, breast, hip, thigh and leg. Above the sound of breaking waves another sound is heard: perhaps, it comes from one, possibly from both, thick, unintelligible and caught somewhere between chest and throat, it straddles a laugh and a cry.

Hurriedly they tear at each other, clothing resists. Then, as if to torment themselves and further taunt their mutual urgency, slowly and with great care they begin to undress each other, until naked and wrapped each around the other, they fall to the ground.

Fingers wander, touch, stroke, sometimes at random, sometimes purposefully; they linger, they trace… breasts, ears, buttocks, lips—there is no order to this twinned and shared search. Against the suck and pull of the surf their sounds become a rhythm, harsh, contrapuntal and wordlessly articulating something old. Yet very new.

A cloud moves to cover the moon, the waves becoming all the louder for the sudden blackness. When moonlight reveals the figures next they are standing still clasped but now more fiercely. The earlier unity appears to struggle violently with and against itself. Abruptly, almost savagely, limbs disengage to become distinct and separate. Where gestures once spoke the language of desire, if not love, bodies now describe harsh and angular hieroglyphs of aggression.

One strikes repeatedly at the other. About the head and what must be the face. Two arms are raised in the moonlight. In self-defence or attack. It is difficult to tell. One runs, the other pursues, catches and throws to the ground that which recently appeared inseparable from it. The assault continues with fists and feet. The figure on the ground struggles—less now than before. An arm is raised and with it a rock or stone—a piece of driftwood, perhaps.

"No! Please! Don't—I'm sorry! I didn't have—" Blows cut short words as skin splits, flesh tears and bone splinters. Blow follows on blow, like the waves in their sameness, regularity and inevitability: it might have been clothes at a riverside that were being pounded for all that it mattered.

Spent and exhausted, the figures become one again. One lies on the other and sobs: its shudders shake the now-still body. In the small night breeze sharp with the smell of brine and rotting seaweed, both bodies cool rapidly. Shivering and still sobbing, one figure rises, rushes into the black sea and completely immerses itself.

In a breeze so slight it barely ripples the black water, white frills on a white skirt move. Their faint disembodied movements imitate the white-edged waves that erupt without cease out of the blackness.

, , ,

Toronto

Why would a rich and beautiful young woman not have a lover? Male or female? Ask yourself that question. That's what I asked Graham de Lisle when I first met him. But then I'm leaping ahead of myself in the telling of this tale, which is not really mine to tell. Or anyone else's, for that matter. Not even the beautiful Ayo's. (Even though de Lisle tried to tell it.)

By way of introducing myself, let me say right off the top that the three things I love most in life are good food, good sex and good hard work, though not necessarily in that order. Work, I suspect, will always be there, although it might not always be the most challenging. Same for good food. After all, I live in a city where I can lie in bed of a morning, stretch my body, curl my toes and say to myself: Today I'm going to eat Japanese. Or, I think it'll be Ethiopian tonight. Or Tibetan, or North Indian. They're all there for the choosing—a sort of world cuisine. Sex, however, is a whole other kettle of fish. Or can of worms. Or whatever metaphor you care to use. I myself prefer ball of wax with all its sticky connotations. Anyway, at best it's unpredictable; at worst there just isn't any—which, by the way, has got to be better than bad sex any day. That being the case, then, you may be wondering what in hell's name I was doing lying in bed next to a snoring man—all right, I grant you it was gentle snoring—after a not-so-good night in bed? Problem is you never quite know what adjective you're going to use after a night in bed, do you? Or even if you were going to need an adjective. First, there's sex, or rather what I call "just sex," which is like your meat and potatoes—solid and satisfying but not overly exciting. Then, there's bad sex, which, as far as I'm concerned, is far better forgotten. The quicker, the better. But good sex! Now *that's* hard to define. And when you and your partner agree on what makes it good, then, simply put, it's just great!

Then again, my idea of good sex might not be anyone else's. My meat, so to speak, might be another's poison. After all, there are some folk who like being tied up and beaten, some like being covered in whipped cream, and there are even those who like being cut. Then, there are the ones who are into fisticuffs and some who are into handcuffs. Not for me any of those delights. I prefer sailing close to the wind and to save my experimentation for food. Don't get me wrong, I'm not your missionary-position type. All I'm saying is that I'm not into swinging from the ceiling. But having said that, I do know good sex when I see it—or rather experience it. It's like a cat recognizing a rat, isn't it? You just know it when you feel it. Like style, it just is, and is more, so much more, than the sum of its parts... or our parts, for that matter. And no, the earth had most certainly not moved for me last night. Not even a teensy-weensy bit. Think about it, the Kama Sutra describes more than fifty positions for sex—fifty-nine to be exact!—and last night I couldn't even find one, not even the missionary. All in all, I was one hell of a dissatisfied woman and wanting to spread some of that dissatisfaction around. But I refrained from turning on the light. Or waking him. Or hitting him on the head. I was going to have me a cigarette instead...

Oh yes, I did say I would introduce myself, didn't I? Obadiah Langford, that's me—or simply Diah to my friends.

The woman rolls over, looks at her sleeping companion and groans. We leave her to find her cigarettes: she has time for one, maybe even two, before she has to get ready for work.

Before going any further I, too, should introduce myself: call me what you will—storyteller, griot, narrator, liar, soothsayer—whatever or however you wish to name me, but I am the one who doesn't know yet does; who speaks yet is silent; who forgets yets remembers. The one they call the unnamed one, and this story is not mine to tell either. I merely speak "on behalf of," remembering the unremembered, speaking the unspeakable, naming the unnameable, which must, all the same, be remembered, spoken and named. And, contrary to all appearances, I am no more able than she is to tell it. Alone, that is. Some stories need many voices: the burden of telling would be too much for one voice, that is. Would, indeed, crush the teller in the telling. As each life is a web of many, many others, so too is this tale.

So, I begin at the beginning. Of this particular story, at least. Which is not at all a beginning, for, indeed, there is no beginning. Or end, either. In the time of no time...

, , ,

LotiaGo

LotiaGo is the name. The name of the time the OroSan calling that time, the time of no time when first they coming running, running from the place where the ones they calling the FunFuns living, running from where the FunFuns working them to death, or killing them with work, is all the same. Is come they coming. Running. Man and woman, boy child and girl child, even baby inside mother and with them the OroSan bringing their hoping and their praying, their fearing and their longing; they bringing with them all the empty spaces inside and outside their bodies where their gods living but long gone from, as well as the remembering of those gods. All the gods they remembering and who remembering them, because the OroSan understanding that is not enough you remembering a god if the god forgetting you...

, , ,

Southampton

The man on the dock watches the containers with his furniture, his books, even his car—all his worldly possessions, in fact—being lifted onto the cargo ship. The SS *Gravenhurst*. It hadn't been easy being allowed on to the loading dock, but through a friend of a friend who knew a chap who knew a chap, here he was—he had wanted to see his things off, why he didn't know.

He had been tempted to leave it all behind. Walk away from it. Begin again. But you could never begin again, could you? And he knew that within a week of arriving at his destination he'd be wanting everything that was familiar around him.

The sound he makes is part sigh, part grunt, remembering how little there was that was familiar to him when he had first arrived some three decades earlier. At this very port. Southampton. He feels a familiar tightening in his chest, not so much pain as an ache for the sapling youth of some eighteen years who had stepped off the gangplank onto the shores of a cold, wet, damp island—was hard to believe that he'd ever been so appallingly, so shockingly naive...

The water, a sullen lead colour, implacably almost preternaturally calm, is a foil to his emotions and thoughts running willy-nilly all over the place. Odd bits of debris float around the ship's hull, the gulls swoop low looking for food. It had been a morning very much like this one when he had arrived from EnIsle, the sky low-slung, dark, ominous even...

A sudden, cold wind blows in from the sea: pulling his coat more closely around him, he walks over to the elderly man who had allowed him to watch the loading, thanks him and leaves. To return to his hotel room where he would stay for the next seven days. In that time he would receive his Decree Absolute of divorce, conclude all his business and financial affairs then leave. God had created the world in six days, so the Bible had said at least, then rested on the seventh. He would unmake his world in seven and leave on the eighth.

, , ,

EnIsle

"Murder! Murder! Murder!"

First one then another news vendor picks up the cry, plays around with it: "Murder in your murder! Murder for so!" then passes it on—"Murder on we island!" But long before the vendors begin competing with each other, in that black, still time islanders call "fore-day-morning," when the only promise of approaching light is the vocal strut of the island's cocks, as each, sometimes in unison, sometimes not, assaults the ambient darkness to champion himself above all others, news of the murder begins its inexorable seep through the villages and towns of the island.

On that particular morning, having summoned the light, the cocks fall, strangely, silent. They rest: the present imperative of silence equal to and balanced by the earlier impulse to sound. In their premature silence, the cocks are, perhaps, anticipating and foreshadowing the fierce competition the morning will bring in the voices of the news vendors. Whatever the reason, by five-thirty that Monday morning, the Caribbean island of EnIsle lay quiet at the halfway point between the clangour of the island's cocks, and the soon-to-be clamour of its vendors.

, , ,

Toronto

Except for the faint early morning light leaking through and around the slats of the shuttered Venetian blinds, the room lies in darkness. To better heighten her sense of touch, the woman closes her eyes and gropes clumsily among the books and tapes on the bedside table: in the still room the crash of falling books is thunderous. The body beside her stirs, but does not waken. So much for trying to be quiet—she had, at least, found her tobacco pouch and cigarette papers. Propped against the headboard of her bed, she quickly tears pieces of tobacco from the pouch, lays them on the paper and rolls it: even in the dark her fingers are quick and skillfull. When she is done, she runs her tongue wetly along the gummed edge of the cigarette paper, gently but firmly turns it down, tamps both ends and smiles with satisfaction at her handiwork. Now, if *only* she had the same sort of control over certain aspects of her life.

With the angular grace of a spider her fingers move, first under the bedside table, then under the bed where they scrabble around stirring up dust in their search for matches. When first her fingers close around the object, she believes it alive, so smooth and pliable is it, with an animal softness almost, then, hot with shame, she quickly withdraws her hand and glances guiltily at her still-sleeping companion. How was she to know it was there? She did sweep occasionally—all right not very often under the bed, but no one looked under beds—God only knew what you might find there. And what she'd just found under her own bed was proof of the correctness of her approach, wasn't it? Ma would have had a fit, though, then a mouthful to say about it. How long had it been lying there? Was it the only one? Ma was watching her, she knew it, wherever she was, and shaking her head at her daughter's sloppy housekeeping habits: "People will judge a book by its cover, chile," she could hear Ma's voice—"And a woman by the house she keeps." She completes the saying (it was one of Ma's favourites), out loud. She was on the slippery slope to damnation and moving fast. And the less Ma knew about her sex life the better... But the condom she'd just found was a dead giveaway, wasn't it? What was she talking about? She didn't have a sex life. Hadn't had one for quite a while. Wasn't for lack of trying, either. Oddly enough, she was far less concerned with Ma's possible disapproval of her sexual life than with her condemnation of her lax and slipshod ways. In the one case Ma was ignorant, at least on the surface, of the details; in the other, she knew only too well her daughter's standards when it came to keeping her living space free of dust balls and dirty dishes. She would be judged. In Ma's court. And found guilty. Of slovenliness. And procrastination.

Hell, all she had to do was thumb through the Yellow Pages and "rent a wife," hire a butler, Molly Maid or Super Susy. Except it wasn't so easy: she didn't want to hire someone white. They were bound to see her untidy habits as an extension of her colour. And she still couldn't bring herself to hire a Black woman. Smoothly, effortlessly the arguments spin themselves into a sticky and familiar web of inextricable logic and irrationality that traps her. Was downright stupid, that's what it was—she, the daughter of a woman who for several years had earned her living cleaning houses, had sworn never to hire someone like her mother. Someone who needed work *and* to be paid a decent wage.

"Is not good enough I cleaning their dirt, chile, but I must be doing it free. Huh! See me crosses in this here lan' they calling Canada." She and her mother are sitting of an evening, as they often do, at the kitchen table in their small apartment above Piazza's Grocery on St. Clair Avenue West in Toronto. It's supper time: Ma is talking, she listening. The anger tightens her vocal chords, flattens the resonant timbre of her voice and makes it high and tinny as she complains about her employers:

"These people don't understand slavery long done and gone."

Then, as often as not, the voice would soften and her eyes become gentle as they focussed on her daughter:

"But you, chile, you having a chance in this here country. Make sure you is you own boss and don't have nobody—white *or* black—telling you how and why you must be doing something."

When Ma graduates from the Registered Nursing Assistant program at George Brown College, she cries. Ma too. It is a spring day of remarkable softness, palpably distant from the harsh cold of winter and the stifling heat of summer, and all the more memorable for it. Eagerly, even prematurely, she had shed her sweaters for a short-sleeved summer dress, the better to expose her limbs to sunlight. But winter dies hard in Canada, lingering on in the body's memory. The skin on her arms, remembering below-zero temperatures, immediately puckers into goose-bumps at a breeze bearing but the faintest hint of a chill. She shivers now as she did back then. Except there is no breeze to account for it. Ma stands framed and double-imaged. Two Ma's! Until she adjusts the lens. She laughs, Ma does, into the eye of the camera; in her arms she carries a large, golden sheaf of daffodils. Long before she ever set eyes on them, Ma has loved daffodils:

"Chile, I used to wonder what 'a crowd, a host of golden daffodils' looking like, with all that 'fluttering and dancing in the breeze'."

Many a night she falls asleep to the words of the poem, especially if Ma doesn't have time to read her a bedtime story: "I wandered lonely as a cloud on high..." The words a part of her now, almost as much as her skin is. "When all at once I saw a crowd, a host of golden daffodils..." As much as Ma is.

"When I first hearing that poem in school, chile, is like everything in me tingling and growing bright bright. That was me own poem, written just for me."

She herself had nothing against Mr. Shakespeare, Ma tells her, but her money was on that Mr. Wordsworth: as far as she was concerned, he was the greatest poet who had ever lived. That was why she had to go to England:

"I wanted to see if that Mr. Wordsworth was right about all the joy he feeling just seeing those flowers, or even just remembering them. "How a flower bringing so much happiness, chile? I just couldn't understand it. It had to be a special kind of flower, and I had to see it with me own two eyes."

When first she sees them, they neither flutter nor dance in a breeze—that would have to wait for another day, another time—but lie very still on a Covent Garden market stall. Reaching out her hand, she touches them as she would the softly beating spot crowning a newborn's head. Gently. Very, very gently. Then, she buys one. One only. A single daffodil to take home and nurture until its yellow withers, becomes sere and crumbles in her fingers.

Had Ma ever found the joy and happiness that "that Mr. Wordsworth" and his daffodils had promised? She didn't know—had never thought to ask. She would have to settle for the image of Ma: Ma in her dark green suit; Ma holding in her arms a great big armful of golden daffodils that she, Diah, had bought to surprise her on her graduation—Ma, perfectly framed and laughing into the eye of the camera. And everything within her now ached to make that image real.

⁊   ⁊   ⁊

LotiaGo

Is long time now the OroSan thinking their gods forgetting them, not helping or saving them from the Funfuns. Until they coming. Running. To the forests of the island people calling EnIsle, the forests where they and their gods coming alive again. Running, they coming with forgotten names and memories they not remembering, and they all coming very much alive again, the ones who forgetting the remembering and the ones they not remembering. The forgetting and the forgotten ones. Is the forests and trees, all the places to be hiding their power, that the gods needing and wanting, the shadowing of light, the rush of river and roar of waterfall, so that their spirits, the same ones that giving length, breadth, depth and height to the very shapes entering them again and giving names to their shapes. But more than anything else, is the mountains the gods longing for, and their forests, to be hiding themselves and their people, the OroSan....

⁊   ⁊   ⁊

London

The man had found himself a room in a very posh hotel in the centre of London. What the natives called the City. The Savoy lived up to its claim of its "unsurpassed London river view." More to the point, it was within walking distance of the Thames: he had wanted—needed—to be close to water. And having decided he would leave in style, unlike the way he had entered, the Savoy's boast of "British style and tradition coupled with innovation" struck the right note. He was not disappointed.

He had left three suitcases in the hotel's storage and had the valet deliver two to his room, one of them an old, battered, brown cardboard case—he still called it a grip—which he now stared at hesitantly, even balefully.

The young man who had first travelled with that grip—he had really only been a boy—still existed somewhere. Maybe locked inside the grip itself. With his index finger he traced his name on the old label glued to the outer side of the grip's lid: Benjamin Osanyin, Magdalene College, Oxford University, Oxford, England. He had written it himself at the bidding of his mother.

Grasping the handle he lifts, feeling the grip's heft. Lighter or heavier? Than when he first arrived? He can't tell. So fiercely does he grip the handle, the suitcase becomes an extension of himself. To remove it from him would require severing his arm from his body. And, standing on the cold, damp Southampton dock, so intense is his longing to fly back home, like Quarshie, who everyone in the village said flew back to Africa every Friday night, he is surprised to find that he hasn't moved after what seems a lifetime. He reads his name on a sign someone holds aloft. It is the only thing he recognizes. Someone welcomes him—the person carrying the sign. He cannot speak. His tongue cleaves to the roof of his mouth.

Many is the time, in those early months after his arrival, he becomes paralysed. Rooted to the spot. Bereft of speech. Some moments brief as the blink of an eye, others as long as the eternity between the exhale and inhale of breath. Whenever he thinks of his mother. Or father. So much so, his adviser recommends he see a psychiatrist. He solves the problem himself: he stops thinking about either of them. Simply erases them from his mind.

Despite their rust, the locks snap open quickly, almost, it seems to him, eagerly. There is still the belt to be undone. He hadn't wanted to but his mother had insisted they secure the suitcase with it. There were no keys for the locks, she had said, and what if the grip flew open during the long journey? His fingers now fumble with the buckle–the aged leather, stiffened and hardened into resistance, initially defies his clumsy attempts to loosen it from the metal's clasp until it appears suddenly to reward his persistence and allows him to unfasten it.

The odour, when he opens the grip, is a familiar one, slighly acrid yet musty, of old papers left too long enclosed. With two exceptions, the clothing and personal items that the grip contained have long since disappeared—sold, given away or lost in his many moves. As if in benediction, his hands hover over the grip's contents. He fingers the yellowed newsprint of the clipppings, slowly shuffling them while trying to remember why he had clipped them in the first place.

The reasons for clipping and keeping the article on the forced repatriation of Black peoples, or the "colour problems" as the newspapers described them, were still relevant even if the stories were no longer topical. But why in heaven's name had he clipped the one on Maypole dancing? Then, as if from a long, long way away, a faint memory stirs within him: in his village they had danced something like the Maypole. A long, long time ago.

A yellowed clipping slips from his fingers and floats to the floor: picking it up he gazes at three pictures of a young girl. One as a baby, the second at five years old and the third at about age ten. The headline reads: "International Baby Seeking Better Home in Canada." He doesn't need to read the article, so clearly does he remember the facts: The girl, one of a pair of twins, had been born on board an Italian ship, the SS *Auriga,* in international waters, to a Kittian mother, a British subject, emigrating to England from the Caribbean. One of the twins, both girls, had died. The surviving one and her mother had been greeted with champagne and flowers when they had finally arrived at Dover via Genoa and Calais. The mother had wanted to know if the flowers—yellow chrysanthemums—were daffodils, only to be told that she would have to wait until the following spring to see daffodils.

Life had not been overly kind to Clarissa and Obadiah Langford in England, the article stated, and after ten years mother and daughter were leaving for Canada "to make a new and better life." The writer wished them the best of luck. One less "colour problem," he remembered thinking at the time.

At the bottom of the suitcase lay the letters, each written on a blue airmail form; collectively they formed an ocean, albeit oblong as oceans are not. An intensely blue ocean that both chronicled and contained his past. They, the letters, most of them unread, were the only remaining and tangible evidence of those early years of his separation. From what, though. Home? He no longer had a home. Anywhere. Nevertheless, he was going Home.

He dips his hand into the sea of blue paper, sifting through the letters as he would sand at a beach. In the beginning he had kept them in chronological order, but whatever order there had been had long since disappeared.

He finds the first letter, received some six months after he had arrived. In it his mother urges him to remember he was leaving the darkness of his former life behind and moving towards the light of education. A British education! He was to make the best of it. He had answered her, enclosing with his letter a map of the Underground. He wanted to show her how much darkness there was in this new land—how people travelled for miles in the darkness, under the ground, no less. He told her that while his new home, England, was very light and bright at times, there was another kind of darkness. He didn't have words for it yet, though. That was when he decided not to mail the letter to her. Someone would have to read the letter to her, and others would know he wasn't happy. She had endured a great deal to send him away; he would not make her life more difficult. So he had remained silent. In the light. And the darkness.

, , ,

EnIsle

By eight o'clock on any morning in EnIsle it would be too late to experience it, but for the two hours immediately before that time, when the light has not yet harshened, but remains gentle, arising as it were from all round, and appears not to have one overhead source; when the sun has not yet hardened the land into contrasts of light and shade and halftones are still visible, the air and light have a quality about them that defies description. Those brave enough to risk it fall immediately into cliché and hackneyed phrase.

It is a time when comparisons, no matter how apt or outrageous, offer little comfort, for none can pin down the essential quality of air or light. You could, however, almost too easily, believe that the air must have had this very quality, this same fresh, clean, sweet smell when Taino, Ciboney, Arawak and Carib, the first peoples, made the island their home. You could argue persuasively with yourself that the first European to claim the island as his own would have smelled air like this; so too would the first African arriving in chains. They would have felt these very breezes, which the travelogues describe as balmy, but which, given the right time of the year, could curdle their balm into winds travelling at more than one hundred miles per hour.

It is a time of day when temperature, humidity, light and landscape all work together to produce words like "Eden," "Paradise," or "God," which the observer, in more cases than not, not wanting to appear sentimental or foolish, will leave unspoken. Simply put, you feel you could die looking at the landscape or breathing the air.

When describing the island, travelogues do not talk of this time, but of scuba diving, birdwatching, sunshine, and white-sand beaches. EnIslers, however, take it for granted, assuming it to be neither different or same the world over: this is the way it is on EnIsle and that is enough.

Between six and eight o'clock on this particular morning, the air is as it has always been, the breezes as balmy as they ever were, or would be; the landscape as capable as ever of stopping the breath. But the aesthetic qualities of their island are far from the minds of the townspeople of Landinam: as they pass through Man O' War Square under the spreading Samaan tree on their way to the various offices and stores that border the square, news of the murder assaults the air with the same brashness and braggadocio the crowing cocks had displayed earlier.

On this particular morning the vitality of the newspaper vendors is at cross-purposes with what they advertise—death. Eight or so news vendors—more than twice the usual number—occupy the square while another half-dozen, at least, are spread out along Calvary Hill leading steeply up to one of the square's entrances. That there is money to be made in the news that morning is not the only reason for the increase in the number of newspaper vendors: there is also the desire to be a part of what is the most exciting event to have happened on EnIsle since Angelina Procope, the sixteen year old daughter of the Moravian minister, eloped with Father Timothy, the young Catholic priest just out from Ireland. That was two years ago.

"Murder in your murder! Murder for so! Murder on we island!" someone shouts.

"If you too small to read, let your Mammy read for you," another answers. "And if you too old and can't see to read, den let the pickney dem read for you!"

Depending on when you pass Man O' War Square on this particular morning, you might hear nothing more than a chant obeying strict antiphonal laws of the African call-and-response tradition, with one vendor singing out her call: "Murder! Murder! Murder on we island!" while another responds:

"Come one, come all, come read 'bout it! read 'bout murder on we island, on beautiful EnIsle!" At other times, however, you will hear a less cooperative, more open type of verbal warfare, as each vendor, trying to outdo the others in wit, vies to be the most outrageous:

"Dis murder bound to turn your hair white when you read 'bout it," followed by a sharp criticism: "If you don't careful, he goin' tief your money!" Along with explicit reasons for buying this particular newspaper from this very vendor: "My news is de most complete news you goin' find anywhere on EnIsle," and—as a lagniappe or bonus—a compliment to the buyer: "But, Missis, what a nice dress you wearing today!" There are times when you can even witness the progression from the pure call and response to the Western hybrid, jazz, as one vendor spotlights his call, while others cut in with their own riffs, calling against yet with each other in a noisy babel of voices and rhythms to create, finally, a sense of unity, harmony even.

As the morning wears on the news begins to lose its novelty, the vendors to cut their refrains with advertisements of other goods that they always carry, forcing news of the murder to compete more and more with the constant appeal of these items: "Murder! Murder! Murder in your murder! Murder on we island! Fine pots and pans, beautiful underwear for the ladies—is murder on we island! C'mon, c'mon, read 'bout it and check out de slippers too!"

Staid, proper and discreet, more British than the British, *The Mercury Standard*, one of the three local dailies, bemoans "the harmful effects of the murder on the tourist industry," predicts a "fall in the GNP and a loss of foreign exchange," while deploring "the loss of old values." Empire is never mentioned, but it casts a long and lingering shadow over the columns of the editorial page.

Talk It and *Off Side*, the other two dailies, each carry large pictures of the victim and compete each with the other for publication of the most lurid and inaccurate details of the victim's life. Beyond the fact that a murder has been committed, not much else is yet known. Lack of information, however, merely fuels the already incendiary imaginations of the reporters. Readers learn that the victim is "from away," and that cocaine, heroin, marijuana, alcohol and sex are all involved in the murder. *Off Side* identifies the victim as a high-class prostitute; *Talk It* as a movie star.

These three dailies all come from the neighbouring island, Belisle, which together with EnIsle form the twin-island state bearing both their names, but, more often than not, colloquially referred to as B&E. The weekly, *EnIsle News*, the only newspaper to be written, printed and published on EnIsle will not be published for another four days. As often happens, EnIslers first get news of themselves from Belisle, and those wanting a more local slant to the news of the murder will have to wait.

If, however, for several nights after the murder, you happened to be awake at midnight, and in the right location on EnIsle, you would have heard the drums, which beat incessantly until the early hours of the morning. You might have asked EnIslers what they meant, to which they might have answered with a shrug and reluctantly told you that it was probably the maroons, the ones who call themselves OroSan, living up in the mountains. And were you to push them further for more details, they might have said that they were either celebrating a birth, mourning a death or praying to their damn foolish African gods. One or two might have added that it had to do with obeah and superstition; others that it was pagan and un-Christian and that it didn't do to ask too many questions.

Gail Scott

Interview with Gail Scott

New York, December 2008[*]

Kate Eichhorn: In the United States, experimental prose has had a somewhat different history than it has had in Canada where, at least in an English-language context, it has been marginalized on the literary terrain. How might we account for this difference, and has your time spent in residency in New York shifted your thinking on this question?

Gail Scott: A huge question. During my residency here in New York, I've found it very nourishing to be among so many formally radical writers. We are a sparser group at home in Montréal. There is an avant-garde prose tradition in the US that is traceable both in New York and along the West Coast back a long way, from Stein, Jane Bowles, Djuna Barnes, through the Beats and the near contemporaries like Kathy Acker, Burroughs—mostly queer by the way—and on up to the present. I don't feel entirely comfortable comparing here to Canada—because I am normally located in Québec and don't extensively know what is happening at the ground level in other regions. But there does exist, pan-continentally, a loose network of experimental prose writing located between the poetry world and the more commercial world of the novel-as-product. People are doing all kinds of weird and wonderful things with the novel in Canada,

---

[*] Excerpt from interview forthcoming in Kate Eichhorn and Heather Milne, eds. *Prismatic Publics: Innovative Canadian Women's Poetry and Poetics*. Toronto: Coach House Books, 2009.

but as far as I know—and this is in part due to demographics—there is not the same depth of commitment to experimental prose. Some writers start out doing amazing innovative work—Michael Ondaatje, to take a famous example—but mellow out at a certain point. Could this be because national identity questions keep popping up in Canada? It's hard to work with a disintegrating writing subject—which is for me what formally distinguishes experimental prose from innovative prose—and cope with national identity issues at the same time. In both countries, the conversation with poetry is crucial for experimental prose writers. In fact, the San Francisco queer New Narrative writers emerged in part as a response to Language writing, while, concomitantly in Québec, as I've said elsewhere, there was a moment of very experimentally formal work, organized around gender issues, more feminist than queer, that paralleled what was happening in San Francisco in the '80s when the New Narrative group emerged. Living here in New York has made it easier to think of myself in that space between poetry and prose that seems to be the most productive for me. I have been going to every reading I can go to at the Poetry Project and at the Segue Series at the Bowery Poetry Club, and that means at least two per week. There is also the excellent Belladonna Series at Dixon Place. And what I have learned about writing since I've been here, I've learned mostly from poets.

KE: There was also the talk you gave at the CUNY Graduate Center. This was an interesting event for a number of reasons. You've talked before about the need to create a space for dialogue on experimental prose writing, and the discussion after your presentation—especially your dialogue with Renee Gladman and Eileen Myles—suggests that other prose writers share your desire to open up such a space. But there was also a slight tension in the room—a sense that the prose writers and poets present were speaking somewhat different languages, approaching questions from somewhat different angles... What happened?

GS: As experimental prose writers, we're used to resistance from some poets—those married to genre, I guess. Living among poets is absolutely essential to our work because it keeps us focused on language. Talking to some fiction writers about the mechanics of our craft leaves me bored out of my mind—the preoccupation with "characterization" and transparency—loses track of the work on language, syntax, complex subjectivities—the stuff of experimental prose investigation. So, while speaking to poets is absolutely essential, I talked to several of the prose writers after the CUNY talk who agreed—we haven't managed to convey the particular problems and issues connected with this kind of work. And the specific space it can actually occupy, which means saying to poets: "Move over a little bit and let us in," but which has also been saying for a long time to the other side of the spectrum, "We're not one of you either." As a group—and it varies very much within the group—the relationship between words, sentences, paragraphs is foregrounded. I experience the sentence, and not everyone experiences the sentence this way—Ron Silliman, for example, doesn't experience the sentence this way—but I do experience the sentence as a sort of problematic summary or look back. The effort of crafting a sentence leads to a moment of closure, I think. I see that space between sentences as an abyss. And it's very hard for me to then traverse that space toward the next sentence—it's actually extremely hard work—projecting a contiguity but not a traditional contiguity, which works something out in relationship to reality, which is not a relationship of trying to mirror reality. Notwithstanding the focus on language, it's not exactly the job that poets are doing. It's not what prose poetry is about either. And it's certainly a different exercise than mainstream fiction.

KE: So where is the line between something like West Coast Canadian writer Fred Wah's prose poems and the type of prose tradition you're locating yourself in relation to?

GS: I don't think there's a line. I think they are all variances springing from similar impulses. Fred is actually one of the people whom I think really understands my work in Canada and whose work I really admire. We have in common complex conflicted backgrounds and a kind of political idealism. I think Fred is more committed to the space of poetry than I am, though he's also a remarkable prose writer. I love the spare yet complex beauty of Fred's work. I write from Montréal, and there's a lot more "packing" in Montréal language and consequently in my prose, because of constant direct interference of the other, or other languages.

You've got layers of language that get squashed together and because, and I hate to repeat this because it has been said so often, but it's true, when you're translating all the time, you keep attempting to grab other moments of meaning or emphasis or noise from the neighbouring language of speech or writing. I experience Montréal as, verbally, a way noisier city than, say, Vancouver, or Edmonton. There is so much talk in the air. That's the way I experience it.

KE: This noise is very apparent in your new work, which you read at the Poetry Project a couple of weeks ago. Here, you have this regionally distinctive architecture, the architecture of the Montréal triplex, holding the novel together in a way, but what is most striking about the work are the multiple layers of language, since in this case, you're working with French, English and Cree.

GS: Well, it's not actually Cree but English spoken by people who a generation or two ago were speaking an Algonquian language. In those passages I read at the Poetry Project, for example, the one about the fly on the plate rail, the accent is the accent I heard in my family, and which I hear from Native people speaking who are fairly close to their original language. The really hard thing about writing this prose work is that I had to set it in Montréal because I don't think I know anything about Native life. I have relatives who are Native, but I have never lived in a day-to-day way on or near a Native community or in a Native context—unless you count time spent with my fairly closeted maternal grandparents. So I had to extend a Montréal context into that thing that exceeds, that cannot be put into words, to torque a phrase from Derrida, talking about the future anterior. I didn't want to do flashbacks. I hate that! I enjoy the challenge of getting something of the effect of a novelistic flashback or reminiscence by torquing language into a composite present. One of the reasons I decided to use film noir as a kind of template for the novel was to be able to avail myself of the device called analepsis—where you are going along, driving along the road, and suddenly you have this black and white insert entering the picture to expose what happened before. The analeptic device proved useful for bringing in these crazy family members from time to time too, plunked in some corner of the Montréal Mile-End flat. It worked to import them to Montréal, because there is the same kind of working class, not terribly confident or aggressive, not really good at the mainstream stuff posture, that I recognize sometimes in members of my own family, and that you can see a lot in East-end Montréal. The triplex frames it all, just like a stage set, and there are all these things going on through the walls and coming up through the floors from the ground under—where once stood Montréal's Crystal Palace, a trope for British colonization, based on the Crystal Palace from the "mother country."

KE: During your reading, after some time, the listener starts to think through the layers. There's a stereoscopic effect.

GS: That's what I'm aiming for. I've been thinking, retrospectively, that I learned this from Gertrude Stein. That is—I realized, reading Ulla Dydo's Stein book, how much Stein had formed my understanding of the relationship between reading and writing. She read Stein and all Stein's archives and notes, a lifetime's worth. And then she wrote a book that said, to grossly re-interpret: When you read Stein, often, you don't necessarily know what is "happening," but after you've finished, you're in her element. It's like a wash—you get all these layers and sounds and colours and vibrations that you may not be able to put into words right away. The effect is astounding. Recently, I was amused, reading *Blood on the Dining-Room Floor*, to see that a certain number of pages in Stein says, if you're confused, go back to the beginning and start over again. Which is often what I want to say to people when they are complaining about the fact that my work is hard to follow. The thing about Stein is that you get meaning but you just don't get it right away. And it's meaning through language, but also as if through music and other forms of composition, as opposed to "meaning" in the usual more direct sense.

KE: You get it through an affective structure as opposed to representation?

GS: Partly. Reading Stein takes you to another dimension in terms of sound, but sound that does not leave the work of language behind. Especially in her really nutty pieces, there's that silly yet riveting nonsensical child voice that goes on. And on. And on. Once you finish reading, even if you don't "follow," you end up in a space that is both affect and thinking. That's what good poetry is like too. You don't necessarily get it from line to line, you don't necessarily feel you have to. With a novel, people feel like they have to get it page by page. Often, in experimental prose, the language work gets left unnoticed in the reader pursuit of instant meaning. Because we are increasingly taught to read thematically.

KE: But what about the place of allegory in your work? Going back to *My Paris*, we see your debt to Benjamin, a great allegorist. Reading Baudelaire recently, I also started to wonder about the influence of Baudelaire on your writing. But Native languages are also deeply allegorical at the level of the sentence, storytelling and rhetoric. How do these connections play out in your new work?

GS: I've only started to think about this recently, because I've been thinking so much about my grandfather, but one thing I distinctly remember about the way he brought me up, and we spent a lot of time with him as kids, is that he would never tell us do or don't. It was always a story, always a story, and it was allegorical. It could be that my love of Benjamin, in this weird way that all these connections come together without your ever knowing it, is also about my love of my grandfather, his stories, the way he talked, which again is very different than my father's side, which is Anglican and Scottish.

KE: I think the convergence of traditions is fascinating. You've gravitated to two very different traditions, or perhaps as you suggest, one led to the other?

GS: I actually think those two traditions have crossed over in Canadian culture a lot more than we realize, and that's one of the reasons I wanted to write this novel. There is a kind of roots tendency in novels where people discover or investigate their heritage. It's not the kind of writing I do. Rather, I am interested in investigating whatever it is that creeps into the language and gestures of people around me, the way they walk, and talk, the way they relate to the world around, from their past and from their immediate context, and that's all really, really good stuff for a prose writer.

KE: I'd like to follow up on a few observations you made earlier—you observed that it's always been the case that a disproportionate number of experimental prose writers are queer. This seems to be true, but is there any way to account for this?

GS: Really, what does queer mean in terms of everyday life? A take on the world? I don't think you can generalize, but since art and eros are closely linked, let's just say I occupy space in a way that is quite distinct from the way space, particularly erotic space, is organized in dominant middle-class heterosexual reality. And let's face it, that latter is the space of an awful lot of novels. Queer implies slippery boundaries. Translate that into the subject of a piece of writing and you can see the piece of writing might well come out differently from say, something David Adams Richards would write. But I don't really understand it. I only know that when I read a novel that involves a heterosexual romance—even though I've written one, though it's also a queer novel because there is also a girl love interest in it—or when I go to a movie or watch a straight love scene on TV, I'm in a foreign country. There is a way that I perceive the world that's outside of that reality, a space which remains essentially socially unstable, and slippy-slidey. Consequently the writing subject speaks à côté. She is constantly re-composing herself. And that makes her utterly contemporary.

KE: I want to return to another issue raised after your talk at the CUNY Graduate Center. Eileen Myles pointed out that there are also many working-class writers who have chosen to work in experimental prose, as if they required a larger canvas to stage their interventions.

GS: Eileen's is the voice of a woman who has nobody sending her cheques for down payments. Added to that is her way of being queer in the world, and the seamlessness she seeks to achieve between the writer and the writing. It's a wonderful project. When I stop to think about it, a lot of us do come from blue collar or lower middle-class backgrounds. Add to that the queer and experimental factors, and perhaps the tendency to be a little desultory is explained. It's a combination of circumstances that sets us up nicely for deconstructing many of the tenets of the novel form. We're trying to be socially ascendant inasmuch as we are trying to get our work out there, but it's a struggle. One of the big issues that a lot of us have is the labour intensity of the work, trying to do what poets are doing in a way and trying to do some of what novelists are doing—it takes twice as much time. So we are a group of people who feel like we should be able to make money from our work like mainstream novelists so we can go on writing eight hours a day, but none of us or few of us do. We're not part of the economy at all, and that's a source of frustration sometimes.

KE: At least if you are an experimental poet, in Canada, you can apply for a grant and your work might be recognized as poetry, but this isn't the case for experimental prose writers. Most fiction juries have no vocabulary, no way of understanding, your work.

GS: True, it's more difficult. As far as those lucrative literary prize dollars, forget it. Erin Mouré once told me I would never win the Governor General's

Award. I don't think it was intended as a criticism of my writing. Virtually every time I apply to the anglophone jury of Le Conseil des arts et des lettres du Québec, I am turned down. I have better luck with the francophone juries. So that points to a difference. I've also had relatively few Canada Council grants. But of course, writers here in the US don't even have those options.

KE: It's a much larger discussion, but the material reality is that doing this work, this kind of writing, is full of risk.

GS: It is. But I started my career as a journalist. I worked as a journalist for about seven years, and I was successful, quite young. I made a lot of money, but I felt like I was participating in something that I really didn't want to participate in. I was telling the truth the best I could, whatever the truth is, but I couldn't really say what I had to say, and I felt cheap, like it was a bad thing to do. Then I thought, okay, I can be successful in a public way if I want, but it's not what I want. I want to do the work I think I should do. That experience made it easier for me than for a lot of people to take those risks—it does make a difference if you've had a little success. I've made the choice to risk failure in market terms. I don't like having so little fruits for my labours, but at least I'm doing what I think I should be doing.

KE: My final set of questions concerns gender and feminism. Your essays in *Spaces Like Stairs* advanced a discourse on feminist poetics. Although it has been over two decades since this collection was published, I continue to meet younger writers in Canada and the US who have read these essays and consider them to be very influential. But I wonder, do you still consider gender and feminism important to discussions of experimental writing?

GS: Let me answer this in a kind of roundabout way. A while ago Lisa Robertson read in Montréal, and this was when she was in California working with Lyn Hejinian at Berkeley, and someone asked her if she was a Language writer now, and she said—I hope I'm not misquoting her: "No, I don't relate to any particular school, except I would say that I am a feminist writer." And I thought, maybe now to say you're a feminist writer is to make a statement about your aesthetics. Maybe it's no longer in danger of being immediately reduced to a posture of political correctness. I'm a feminist and a writer, so does that make me a feminist writer? Having been through the left, and been involved in a lot of discussions on art and politics, I agree with the idea that an artist needs, as Trotsky and Breton put it in their famous manifesto: *toute licence en art*. If you're a feminist, and you care about women, it's going to show in your work, but I don't think about it in terms of talking in the first instance to women, for example, as I did as a very young writer. And which was a very heady experience. It gave me permission to express my wildness. To experiment, to shout, to play. It's just who I am, and above all, feminism is a big part of why I am as interested in form as I am.

KE: In nearly all the essays in *Spaces Like Stairs* you write about subjectivity. There is a subject-in-process, a subject becoming, but it's still a female subject. It's still a very gendered subject. The "sutured subject" investigated in the paper you presented at the CUNY event represents a shift for you—it seems to be beyond gender.

GS: One thing that I think some poets don't get is that there is a way in which experimental prose writers work on questions of subjectivity very much like poets do. In other words, the subject is very much embedded in language, as opposed to having a subject you want to represent from the outset. The word sutured is very important because there is a way of faking sewing all of it all back together again in all kinds of weird and wonderful ways to make it imply "story," but the subjectivity that gets projected is not some mirror version of a supposed reality. It's like Humpty Dumpty. Who needs to be put back together again. But how? I had this intuition all along. I remember in *Spaces Like Stairs*—and a lot of those pieces were polemics, written as interventions for conferences or debates with other women writers—but even then, I was aware of not wanting a certain pc notion of feminism or any political notion to close down the writing. What I like about the notion of queer, I guess, is that it operates back and forth over cusps between gender impulses or between any impulses. The fly, in this new book, is both a guy and her alter ego, a good solution for a "femme" sort of lesbian. I'm interested in all kinds of cusps—where gender impulses meet, where languages meet, et cetera.

"MACBETH PHYLETIC" *from* THE OBITUARY

Gail Scott

MACBETH PHYLETIC*

1. THANE OF WRITTEN TROUBLES OF THE BRAIN

MacBeth, therapist, looks out. Splotchy Celtic-French face with touch of Huron in it. Splendidly framed in steel curved-at-th'-corners casement. Th' only late-deco window remaining in this revivalist dump. By April, his cozy little office ~~will have been~~ TO BE [he hates th' future anterior] requisitioned. For language college under. Entoutkàs, th' place already ruined [here, MacBeth makes a mou]… Save, dieu merci, stair-rail's sleek gold horizontal arrows, winding round oval plaster corners painted *quelle horreur* baby blue. But

Who's that knocking at th' gate?

Through faint-grey tinted pane. Low *in-grate* buildings. Restaurant supplies. Tuxedos. Weddings. Leopard Costume Rentals. Traffic, ave. du Parc: souped, battered, glittery or ratty, 20 percent junky, you can tell by th' shuffle. *Whom we, for peace, have treated poorly.* His favorite client's late. —*Your option*—he telling her. Yet wishing to

Cure her of that!
Canst thou not minister to a mind diseas'd
Pluck from th' memory a rooted sorrow
Raze out th' written troubles of th' brain?—

At least she's fairly named: *Rose*. Notwithstanding th' practice, in different regions, of naming little twats variants thereof: Rosella in Bouctouche; Ro-zanne in Ste-Bonne; Rose Rose in Hoche-Maison; Rosine [she ultimately asserting] after old postcard in ~~Grandpa's~~ Veeera's drawer of Wiertz's *La Belle Rosine*. Talking pleasantly with her skeleton. Th' therapist, globe in his hand [to keep from washing them again], twirling on heel + sitting [gingerly] at parabolic amber École des meubles de Montréal desk. And being—man both frivolous + metaphysical—copying in minuscule script in minuscule moleskin of th' type used by Hemingway + co. From platinum laptop monitor:

I/Rosine hiking in Puerto Barrida. Incredible green cliffs plunging to sea. Narrow path along precipice. I am suffering from vertigo. Afraid X [you bitch], prancing like mountain goat behind, will push me off. This fear, irrational.

Straightening [nothing aging like poor posture], the shrink's raising a scratchy cheek. Trousered in sybaritic British tweed, baggy at knees. Against th' smoky window: crackling of leaves. He's loving how Météo Québec showing th' coming pluie glaçante as tiny acute triangles.

Writing [wanting to wash hands]:

Absence per se, not the essence of a tragedy. True, with every libidinal throe preceding the exquisite moment of passing, pleasure's performed as pain. The question being, in the case of the dissociate, or of any child having parents whose talk not complementing th' interior who-am-we: What part of her at any [usually erotic] instigation crossing the great divide? What part [if any] left to speak?

Raising another cheek + listening: no footsteps—only distant yé-yé radio in baby blue hall. He writes:

She's a fake. Like everyone in this place.

2. EYES INCARNADINE, DEVILISH

MacBeth looks down. Avenue du Parc: gas station, hamburger joint, faux-deco *Collège Socrate* [*FRANÇAIS, ANGLAIS, GRECQUE, ITALIEN, ESPANGOL*], cement block refugee-hotel opposite, latest crop of arrivals, lounging out in front.♥ It is autumn. Th' sidewalk blowing with yellow leaves

---

♥ Such covens exist in every city, their insides (like in dreams) partitioned off illegally, into cubicles or cages, whose "walls", for reasons of aeration, not quite up to ceiling. Raising the general erotic ambience to sizzling, a situation the locals not above exploiting. An artist of our acquaintance, tall, willowy, taken one afternoon in flagrant délit with Somalian lover by younger also local chick in taffeta, little rousse couettes, screaming over "wall": lâche donc mon homme.

from parc opposite. Th' globe in his hand. A client entering. Behind. Aubergine dye-job typical of hags in the 'hood. Purse tight under arm. Settling imperiously in his gently contoured École des meubles de Montréal leather-backed chair. He knew her father. A predator. A paranoid. Prodigious energy of shady entrepreneur who, after nombreuse famille asleep, slipping off to bathhouse establishment opposite Little Children of Jesus' Latino-inflected wedding-cake façade with famous rare adolescent Jesus gazing straight over Little-Children-of-Jesus Square. Into steamy bathhouse windows, whose recessed blue door endlessly opening to delectable youths strolling nonchalantly off street. Not to mention th' rapid left-right glance step-glide of older married guys. Th' father, pockmarked like his infamous port-syndicate boss uncle Fred Ball, putatively linked to th' West-end mob. Now she's crossing her knees, lax second-hand linen slacks [—*go shopping, bitch*—], shoulders low, back, hurling with th' unself-consciousness of th' entitled:

—*If you could see what's going in + coming out!*—

MacBeth sits, unwashed hand, for anchorage, on École des meubles desk's substantial amber calf. Face inscrutable, thanks to orange backlight from window. She has shapely lips [he has to admit]. Mouth part open. In speaking, never purses, thus guarding softness of frontal contour. Tongue coming out when disgusted. Ugh—a fat thing. A rat.

—Jo, I understand you want it nice when you retire from th' farm. And come back here to live. Plus, you're mad at your sister. Who on a sunny day moved out and left you th' trouble. Your heart is broken. It's your investment. Conrad warned you about real estate—

—*All night screeching like banshees. Also, washing sex toys on the balcony. That fat shaved guy in leather. Tub. Apron. Dildo like a stallion's. Who's she think she's kidding?*—

—Maybe you have in common—

—*I can get her out if I want. For now, I am tending my garden*—

MacBeth glances round. At dirty avenue, under. In-grate, he repeating: th' only prime real estate facing airy Royal-Mount opposite: chrome-+-plate glass MacRonald's. Giving way immediately to flat-topped diners, sketchy dépanneurs, Dairy Kings, etc. Th' treetops of our Lady of Snowy Angels cemetery, rising beyond. Extending toward Shaaar Hashimoyin, whose peaceful fuchsia-tinted vistas meandering between their close-set stones, th' most peaceful-cause-tasteful spot in th' city. Waiting for her to speak. Globe in hand again. Turning tartly in direction of alley. Th' backs of stacked flats rectangularly framing 3-sided narrow courts, too close, promiscuous. Already at 6 this morning, one of those nosy upper-floor biddies, th' one with th' mouse in her purse, watching him progressing South, accompanying th' incredible lover from

Flatbush to bus [pause for revering lover's scented dreads + cheeky butt, a dancer in fact]. Th' nosy parker[♥] in upper window, canary on thumb, screaming like supporting actress in some Hitchcock thriller: —*Going to be a scorcher*—

The client: —*I was collecting for the co-op*—*not to mention trying to squeeze some rent*—*she's answering th' door, wiggling ass + provoking*: —Hey, you know Louis Riel°°, before you Anglos hanging, living five blocks over?—*I loaned her* Th' Book of Genocides. *To show her. What I know. She tore it. Fortunately for her, not yet a collectible*—

Carefully he stands, commemorating, with surreptitious pat, th' cat o' nine tails last night dexterously applied to ass. Eyeing, Down Below, two handsome [i.e. emaciated] players, pencil-thin denims, three-days' growth, nervy, likely mean-when-unavoidable, gesticulating on filling-station bench. He waits, th' fading red-orange autumn ray powdering baize padded wall opposite. He waits. Silence. Now she's bringing

---

♥ The expression speaks for itself: pure-wool, conjuring a hand-knit sock or mitten, glowing un-self-consciously with irony. For any family tree going back to the early French-speaking settlers includes some Irish [same parish] + frequently, Huron, Abenaki [Algonquin], or Innu [Montagnais], not to mention Polish, Shetland Island, etc. So , "pure laine"—until recent massive waves of immigration—ultimately mostly indicating mother tongue: Québecois French.

up her Grandmother. Born in bottom flat, 4997 Settler-Nun, ca 1921. So you own it all, he ruminating. Bitterly. Entoning, dulcetly: "You told me about her. Sitting on a kitchen chair on balcony, a paper in some script not quite—you often pointing out—European. Unfolding on massive flowered lap—obviously covering some desire you Jo incapable of offering to yourself. The client, thumbs inverted, blurting:

—*The tenant on the second, Leda, clean, nice to the children, had to tell one, so anorexic, heart-shaped glasses, mules, making such a racket skipping non-stop up and down the outside iron stairs:* Vamoose! *The ground-floor Potter, coming herself from Portland, saying crystal meth for sure...*

—So? Escapes from his lips—

MacBeth sits gingerly. Noting in his minuscule script: *In the prolonged absence of the love object, the obsessive turns against her environment.* He sighs, trying to be nice:

—You know, dear Jo, first impressions can be false. Be that as it may, a ~~tooth~~ [he means truth] can sometimes get extracted. Remember how things went beautifully after you at first moved, leaving your flat to Ms. Dousse: The vacation. Fall. Winter. Holes, pimples, blackheads utterly forgotten. Already, from down the street. You were loving Rosine, your new tenant's curly little head. She was your replacement.

—*You're crazy. Like my mother*—

He looks out again. Wondering why women suffer more from ruminations, anxieties, petty quarrels, fatigue + depression. *The soul that in life did not its divine right/Acquire, has not even in Hades, repose* (hölderlin). In five, th' phone will ring. Lover, calling from Flatbush, before going off to pick up his regular. Further out in Brooklyn: He loves him. MacBeth's finger, nail not quite impeccable, being still perfumed with the hole of the other, swiping rapidly by nostril:

—Jo, to think about this week: You a gardener, are weeping over her silver bells, her cockleshells, her pretty maids. In a row—

—*For this I am paying*—

—I'd beg you, don't lean out the window. But with you, there's no danger—

She likes it. Snapping purse + clasping under armpit. The green baize door slamming mutely after lax second—hand linen—slack behind. In minuscule letters in th' minuscule moleskin, MacBeth's noting: *What then is the pleasure of a discourse. In which one no longer means:* Courage, Camille?

He waits.

He waits [mouse scurrying in wall].

3. BUT WEARING HEART SO WHITE

MacBeth looks out. Framed in steel geometry of proto-deco window. Directly over *Collège Socrate* pennants: *FRANÇAIS. GRECQUE. ANGLAIS. ESPAGNOLE. ALLEMAND. ITALIEN. RUSSE.* Scoping th' dark-skinned French-immersion lovelies. Exiting th' building. His own skin—save spots high on cheeks from papa's Celtic predilection for liking his booze—likewise very smooth. Indeed, in profile resembling classy deceased object of th' graffiti. Scrawled under side-alley window: *Trudeau Rapace!*♥. Looking down again. Th' busty girls 're hustling out Collège Socrate door: big earrings, lacy embroidered mules, in style this year, linge très blanche. Knowing how to fold a shirt, *you bet*! He, Étienne MacBeth, is shocked he thinking that. Really. Wanting nothing from "them."

A dozen tiny planes, buffeted by wind, grasshop up above, one, then another, through spotless blue—save odd fluffy cloud—sky. A laundry ad, you could say.

Another client late.

He waits. Hand placed on stomach. Full of th' empties.

♥ Pierre-Elliott Trudeau, or PET°, the Prime Minister so adored by anglos. And hated by franco Québecois for saying Canada not bi- but multi-cultural, making French non-exclusive, i.e. in danger. (°The acronym, in French, onomatipedically sounding: fart).

Th' tweedy knees of his trousers bending to scope left. At large "~~coolie-hatted~~" [phrase repressed immediately] Asian. Leaning over green recycling bin. Is not this acerbity in stomach less *attribuable* to coffee [excellent Armenian torrefacteur's Ethiopian Yergecheffe espresso]. Than to letter from that arrogant Wilman's lawyer over courtyard. Charging him, MacBeth, with harassment, following th' sleepless psychoanalyst's carefully worded missive re: muffling th' terrier. Face—splotches empurpling again—what makes those bastards think they're so entitled? Like Israelis in Palestine. Then

Someone saying: Wilman a Dane.

I'm a racist, he thinking, somewhat disconsolately spreading endlessly washed fingers. Over dilating tummy. Conjuring—scire facias—th' missing Rosie. With her it's not work. *always Bringing news, filling from crown to toe full of direst amusement.* Their collective burning mouths close above his amber desk. Recounting, in voices pretending to be hoarse from secrets + feuilletons: th' proclivities of acquaintances. Last week, th' Potter—MacBeth shrinks them all—heard through front court window —*Having sex for a change! Oooomph,* Rosie laughing… *Ooomph… I was waiting for more. But already it was over*—

Hardly seeming—MacBeth riposting—worth th' effort.

Gazing sideways, th' tinny blue sky's turning hard silver—grey, behind racket of billboards, behind fibreglass siding covering several formerly fantastical old cornices + pediments, ordered, turn of 20th, from San Francisco catalogues. No more fluffy clouds. Nor little grasshopper planes. One helium balloon. Hanging low over th' wingspread angel on th' old carpetbagger Father of Confederation George Cartier's monument. Which monument chain-fenced + swathed in white. To keep th' tam-tams out. *Oh*

Why—he snickering—*have ye clad me in the clothes of others?*

On dark edge of parc, a Thin Man high-stepping. Clearly from dehydration. Eclipsing with little paper bag of syringes [MacBeth almost certain]. Toward bevelled glass façaded washrooms at mountain's foot. Th' blonde cleaner girl, her red municipal truck surely parked out front, this time of day, holding mop + honking. Honking. To get th' users out. MacBeth consults his watch.

L'horloge ne dort pas.

But Thin Man—contrarily, unexpectedly—back-channelling across perspective in weird peripatetic dance. Obsequiously contourning slatted garbage receptacle overflowing with horribly reeking plastic dog-shit baggies. Cop car in passim, ignoring. Th' featured crime this week: unleashed puppies. Riling up th' doggy crowd. Complaining in awful anglo-accented French th' real problem: syringes lurking in th' grass. —*It's our parc. Get the homeless out—It's the city's!*—franco cop retorting to soccer Mom. Further whining patients from Hotel-of-God hospital, IVs in arms, copping hits at parc's south end. —*Wheeling hospital paraphernalia behind!!*—

MacBeth opens a parabolic drawer: Rosie, unseen for a week. Unseen today again. *Halfway between melancholia + paranoia*, he writes in his minuscule book. *Not being authorized to mourn, leaning increasingly toward latter. She thinks she's being watched, when more likely watcher: she*—

From th' drawer with floral locket, th' therapist's selecting bowl-locked Miss Kitty pipe. Grass. Grass of th' parc. Instantaneously greener. Autumn leaves more orange, flying booted toes of fast sashaying girl Down Below, tight blue salopette, good French bangs [her tight little undies blowing somewhere on line]. Holding hand of t-shirted six-packed dude. Dropping, she's forging ahead into two-way traffic of stoners, chiefly Blokes♥ with characteristic toe-out bedroom— slipper shuffle; albeit one Innu disguised as Mexican in sombrero, panhandling by Banque Nationale, one Arab, head nodding, very dark eye circles, sliding onto bench by low gas

---

♥ Term used by francophones over time to indicate "anglo". Generally understood to imply "square heads". Anglo term for franco? *Pepsi*!

station yard brick wall. Th' junior women cops on corner keeping backs pointedly to scene. Very clean shirts, blonde bobs or tails. Sun glinting off solid pairs of waistbelt cuffs, Rosie's preferred accessory. *Now* she saying then speaking so fast she brutally destroying syntax. Punctuation + the right adjectives meaning nothing. Breathlessly assaulting her visual, auditory, olfactory representations, th' steam-rush of emotion bursting every clamp of restraint, her sole preoccupation being to render every vibration of hour with woman-in-uniform under High River bridge in Haeckville, AB. Who first placing revolver on dash, then cuffing Rosine to wheel, et cetera.

Below, heavy post-meridiem grid of shiny metal bubbles. Creeping noisily over macadam. Speaking of "syntax" [hand still on stomach, possibly whoozy from yesterday's incomparable afternoon with th' dancer from Flatbush. Whose singing ass on very white sheets. He worshipping immoderately]. Th' therapist getting up from desk. And dancing little step to th' dub music in head. Feeling [though pushing 50] pretty cool. *Would you dance with me in public?* He asking lover, who replying cautiously: *That depending where.* Down in alley: still no client. Only fat kid pissing on *Trudeau-Rapace* graffiti. And enthusiastic woman shouting confidentially to neighbour:

> *Tomorrow we are having*
> *Chili-encrusted salmon.*

MacBeth writes in tiny little book: *Dispersal: a mental state—related to paranoia—emanating punctually from over-focus on consumption; also known as accident [failure to acquire] avoided.*

Obviously this client. Also not showing.

He lights his little Miss Kitty odourproof paraphernalia. And takes a toke. Are not all paranoids self-fulfilling prophecies? He puts th' bowl-locked odour-discreet Miss Kitty pipe back in drawer.

Someone knocking at door.

*Excerpted from the novel, *The Obituary*.

**Louis Riel, leader of the Métis (French/Cree) Rebellion, late 1800s.

BELLADONNA*

Mary Burger * Camille Roy * Kristin Prevallet * Cecilia Vicuña * Eleni Sikelianos * Fanny Howe * Laura Mullen * Beth Murray * Mei-mei Berssenbrugge * Laura Wright * Lisa Jarnot * Kathleen Fraser * Rachel Blau DuPlessis * Nicole Brossard * Lee Ann Brown * Adeena Karasick * Aja Couchois Duncan * Lila Zemborain * Cheryl Pallant * Lynne Tillman * Abigail Child * Deborah Richards * Norma Cole * Jocelyn Saidenberg * Gail Scott * Carla Harryman * Anne Waldman * kari edwards * Bhanu Kapil * Rosmarie Waldrop * Tina Darragh * Chris Tysh * Jennifer Moxley * Zhang Er * Tonya Foster * Lauren Gudath * Alice Notley * Caitlin McDonnell * Eileen Myles * Suzanne Wise * Lydia Davis * Elaine Equi * Maggie Nelson * Summi Kaipa * Julie Patton * Joan Larkin * Minnie Bruce Pratt * Anne Tardos * Michelle Naka Pierce * Veronica Corpuz * Leslie Scalapino * Jen Benka * Susan Briante * Joanna Fuhrman * Nada Gordon * Catherine Daly * Caroline Bergvall * María Negroni * Lourdes Vásquez * Sasha Watson * Henri Michaux * Genevieve Bernstein * Sandra Moussempés * Jean-Michel Epistallier * Paul Eluard * Joyce Mansour * Oscarine Bosquet * Sabine Macher * Nathalie Quintane * Jaimy Gordon * Rachel Daley * Latasha N. Nevada Diggs * Joan Retallack * Renee Gladman * Eileen Tabios * Susan Howe * Corina Copp * Lyn Hejinian * Mercedes Roffé * Mónica de la Torre * Erín Moure * Lisa Robertson * Martine Bellen * Karen Weiser * Belleza y Felicidad * Mairéad Byrne * Stacy Szymaszek * Nathalie Stephens * Rachel Zolf * Kathe Izzo * Kim Rosenfield * Ann Lauterbach * Myung Mi Kim * Laura Elrick * Melissa Buzzeo * Dawn Lundy Martin * Sharon Mesmer * Marjorie Welish * Laynie Browne * Rae Armantrout * Fernanda Laguna * Gabriela Bejerman * Cecilia Pavón * Elizabeth Willis * Kate Colby * a. rawlings * Margaret Christakos * Deborah Meadows * Laura Moriarty * Rosa Alcalá * Marcella Durand * Akilah Oliver * Erica Hunt * Sawako Nakayasu * Kiriu Minashita * Kyong-Mi Park * Ryoko Sekiguchi * Takako Arai * Patricia Spears Jones * Maureen Owen * Rebecca Brown * Anna Moschovakis * Evie Shockley * E. Tracy Grinnell * Carol Mirakove * Harriet Zinnes * Maggie O'Sullivan * Stacey Levine * R. Erica Doyle * Fiona Templeton * Elizabeth Robinson * Barbara Cole * Tracie Morris * Jean Day * Kathy Lou Schultz * Simone White * Dodie Bellamy * Kevin Killian * Robert Glück * Sarah Schulman * Tisa Bryant * Chris Kraus * Susan Bee * Marjorie Perloff * Emma Bee Bernstein * Johanna Drucker * Jennifer Scappettone * Etel Adnan * Kate Eichhorn * M. NourbeSe Philip